Search and Seizure

Search and Seizure

Martha Bridegam, J.D.

SERIES CONSULTING EDITOR
Alan Marzilli, M.A., J.D.

CHELSEA HOUSE PUBLISHERS

A Haights Cross Communications ✦ Company ®

Philadelphia

CHELSEA HOUSE PUBLISHERS

VP, New Product Development Sally Cheney
Director of Production Kim Shinners
Creative Manager Takeshi Takahashi
Manufacturing Manager Diann Grasse

Staff for SEARCH AND SEIZURE

Executive Editor Lee Marcott
Editorial Assistant Carla Greenberg
Photo Editor Sarah Bloom
Production Editor Noelle Nardone
Series and Cover Designer Keith Trego
Layout 21st Century Publishing and Communications, Inc.

A Haights Cross Communications ⚓ Company ®

http://www.chelseahouse.com

First Printing

1 3 5 7 9 8 6 4 2

Library of Congress Cataloging-in-Publication Data

Bridegam, Martha Ann.
   Search and seizure/Martha Bridegam.
     p. cm.—(Point/counterpoint)
   Includes bibliographical references and index.
   ISBN 0-7910-7487-0 (hardcover)
   1. Searches and seizures—United States—Juvenile literature. I. Title. II. Point-
counterpoint (Philadelphia, Pa.)
KF9630.B75 2005
345.73'0522—dc22

                                                2005000350

CONTENTS

Foreword

Alan Marzilli, M.A., J.D.
Durham, North Carolina

The debates presented in POINT/COUNTERPOINT are among the most interesting and controversial in contemporary American society, but studying them is more than an academic activity. They affect every citizen; they are the issues that today's leaders debate and tomorrow's will decide. The reader may one day play a central role in resolving them.

Why study both sides of the debate? It's possible that the reader will not yet have formed any opinion at all on the subject of this volume—but this is unlikely. It is more likely that the reader will already hold an opinion, probably a strong one, and very probably one formed without full exposure to the arguments of the other side. It is rare to hear an argument presented in a balanced way, and it is easy to form an opinion on too little information; these books will help to fill in the informational gaps that can never be avoided. More important, though, is the practical function of the series: Skillful argumentation requires a thorough knowledge of *both* sides—though there are seldom only two, and only by knowing what an opponent is likely to assert can one form an articulate response.

Perhaps more important is that listening to the other side sometimes helps one to see an opponent's arguments in a more human way. For example, Sister Helen Prejean, one of the nation's most visible opponents of capital punishment, has been deeply affected by her interactions with the families of murder victims. Seeing the families' grief and pain, she understands much better why people support the death penalty, and she is able to carry out her advocacy with a greater sensitivity to the needs and beliefs of those who do not agree with her. Her relativism, in turn, lends credibility to her work. Dismissing the other side of the argument as totally without merit can be too easy—it is far more useful to understand the nature of the controversy and the reasons *why* the issue defies resolution.

The most controversial issues of all are often those that center on a constitutional right. The Bill of Rights—the first ten amendments to the U.S. Constitution—spells out some of the most fundamental rights that distinguish the governmental system of the United States from those that allow fewer (or other) freedoms. But the sparsely worded document is open to interpretation, and clauses of only a few words are often at the heart of national debates. The Bill of Rights was meant to protect individual liberties; but the needs of some individuals clash with those of society as a whole, and when this happens someone has to decide where to draw the line. Thus the Constitution becomes a battleground between the rights of individuals to do as they please and the responsibility of the government to protect its citizens. The First Amendment's guarantee of "freedom of speech," for example, leads to a number of difficult questions. Some forms of expression, such as burning an American flag, lead to public outrage—but nevertheless are said to be protected by the First Amendment. Other types of expression that most people find objectionable, such as sexually explicit material involving children, are not protected because they are considered harmful. The question is not only where to draw the line, but how to do this without infringing on the personal liberties on which the United States was built.

The Bill of Rights raises many other questions about individual rights and the societal "good." Is a prayer before a high school football game an "establishment of religion" prohibited by the First Amendment? Does the Second Amendment's promise of "the right to bear arms" include concealed handguns? Is stopping and frisking someone standing on a corner known to be frequented by drug dealers a form of "unreasonable search and seizure" in violation of the Fourth Amendment? Although the nine-member U.S. Supreme Court has the ultimate authority in interpreting the Constitution, its answers do not always satisfy the public. When a group of nine people—sometimes by a five-to-four vote—makes a decision that affects the lives of hundreds of millions, public outcry can be expected. And the composition of the Court does change over time, so even a landmark decision is not guaranteed to stand forever. The limits of constitutional protection are always in flux.

These issues make headlines, divide courts, and decide elections. They are the questions most worthy of national debate, and this series aims to cover them as thoroughly as possible. Each volume sets out some of the key arguments surrounding a particular issue, even some views that most people consider extreme or radical—but presents a balanced perspective on the issue. Excerpts from the relevant laws and judicial opinions and references to central concepts, source material, and advocacy groups help the reader to explore the issues even further and to read "the letter of the law" just as the legislatures and the courts have established it.

It may seem that some debates—such as those over capital punishment and abortion, debates with a strong moral component—will never be resolved. But American history offers numerous examples of controversies that once seemed insurmountable but now are effectively settled, even if only on the surface. Abolitionists met with widespread resistance to their efforts to end slavery, and the controversy over that issue threatened to cleave the nation in two; but today public debate over the merits of slavery would be unthinkable, though racial inequalities still plague the nation. Similarly unthinkable at one time was suffrage for women and minorities, but this is now a matter of course. Distributing information about contraception once was a crime. Societies change, and attitudes change, and new questions of social justice are raised constantly while the old ones fade into irrelevancy.

Whatever the root of the controversy, the books in POINT/ COUNTERPOINT seek to explain to the reader the origins of the debate, the current state of the law, and the arguments on both sides. The goal of the series is to inform the reader about the issues facing not only American politicians, but all of the nation's citizens, and to encourage the reader to become more actively involved in resolving these debates, as a voter, a concerned citizen, a journalist, an activist, or an elected official. Democracy is based on education, and every voice counts—so every opinion must be an informed one.

———————————————

This volume examines the often difficult balance between law enforcement and civil liberties. It covers the topic of search and seizure, generally meaning searching people, places, and vehicles; seizing property; and arresting or otherwise detaining people. The U.S. Constitution places limits on search and seizure, but the scope of these limits is a frequent topic of public and legal debate. In addition to providing a concise overview of the development of the law of search and seizure, this volume examines the arguments of civil libertarians and proponents of "law and order" relating to current controversies. The major topics covered are excluding evidence on "technicalities," racial profiling, and police misconduct. Special attention is given to the impact of the "War on Terror" on search and seizure law.

Search and Seizure: A Brief Review

This book explores some controversies surrounding official investigations and arrests in the United States. Its title comes from the Fourth Amendment to the U.S. Constitution, which provides:

> The right of the people to be secure in their persons, houses, papers and effects, against unreasonable searches and seizures, shall not be violated, and no warrants shall issue, but upon probable cause, supported by oath or affirmation, and particularly describing the place to be searched, and the persons or things to be seized.

In the amendment's formal eighteenth-century language, the word *seizure* means both the seizure of persons (detaining or arresting people) and the seizure of things (collecting evidence or impounding property).

The Constitution, including the Fourth Amendment, is the supreme law of the United States, so the Supreme Court's interpretation of this amendment has a tremendous effect on police conduct everywhere in the country. It is not the only important law affecting search and seizure, however, nor is it the only one addressed in this book. More generally, the debates analyzed here concern the events that draw a person into the criminal justice process—from the police decision to focus on a particular place, offense, or suspect, to investigations and arrests, to the sort of courtroom objections that are used to allege illegal behavior by the police themselves. Readers will need to look elsewhere for the equally important discussions of prosecutors' decision making, criminal trials as a whole, sentencing, imprisonment, supervised release programs, and the eventual return of ex-convicts to society.

This book is not a criminal defense manual, nor is it intended as advice on how to handle an actual encounter with police. Anyone who is being treated with suspicion in a real criminal investigation should consult a competent attorney as soon as possible—if not on a private basis, then through a non-profit or public defender program—before making any decisions or statements.

In this book, criminal justice issues are presented in terms of legal policy, history, and politics, with the goal of helping readers participate more knowledgeably in public discussion of the role of police agencies. Such discussion has become urgent in a country that, as of 2001, had more than 2 million people incarcerated[1] and that, since the September 2001 terrorist attacks, has intensely debated whether it is consistent with democratic citizenship to increase the powers of police and security agencies.

The street-level realities of U.S. criminal procedure can seem to mock the elegant and seemingly idealistic pronouncements about individual liberty that restrain the law of the United States through the Bill of Rights, the first ten amendments to the Constitution. Police departments are not, and never have been, run by philosopher-statesmen in powdered wigs. The practical application of the criminal law was a scruffy, frequently unfair business at the time the United States was founded. Criminal justice still is scruffy and frequently unfair, although long years of protest and negotiation have gentled some aspects of the process.

What does it mean for police and security agencies to obey the Constitution in their treatment of individuals under criminal suspicion? Civil rights lawyers argue that the U.S. criminal justice establishment has never met its duty to handle suspects as though they were truly presumed innocent until proven guilty. Advocates for a "law and order" perspective often argue that too much concern for accused parties during the past four decades has neglected the rights of crime victims and allowed dangerous people to walk free.

Advocates for "law enforcement"—by which is generally meant the efficient control of crime—sometimes condone violations of suspects' constitutional rights, although the Constitution is the supreme law of the land. Conversely, advocates who feel that the U.S. legal system is stacked against poor and minority individuals have successfully built egalitarian cases on that very system's founding documents. Liberals who have been stereotyped as wanting to leave tradition behind find themselves invoking the 1791 ratification of the Bill of Rights to defend constitutional restraints on police conduct that the Supreme Court only imposed pervasively in the 1960s. Conservatives, stereotyped as opposing "big government," can find themselves defending unprecedented police intrusions into private life.

The traditions of professional state and local policing developed in the United States without much reference to the Bill of Rights, which was at first seen as applying only to federal laws and officials. It was not until the 1868 passage of the Fourteenth Amendment that rights to "due process of law" and "equal protection of the laws" were formally applied to state and local officials' conduct. It took longer for due process and equal protection rights to have real effects on criminal suspects' rights. Court objections about local police violations of constitutional rights did not succeed substantially until the early twentieth century, and it was only about 40 years ago that the real head-on collision between daily police practices and court interpretations of the Bill of Rights began. The reverberations from this collision—which is sometimes remembered as the criminal procedure revolution—are still making themselves felt in courtrooms around the country.

The Warren Court—the Supreme Court sitting under Chief Justice Earl Warren in the 1960s—issued interpretations of a 200-year-old document that imposed new restrictions on long-accepted police methods in a manner that some police officials and their supporters saw as a break with tradition. Each side, in its way, thus claimed to be upholding time-honored ideas of justice, and, in a way, each side was right.

This dispute has become an important part of the perpetual high-stakes argument among political and legal advocates over the lessons of the American past—an argument that has important present-day consequences. The whole U.S. system of government is, after all, restrained by the Supreme Court's interpretation of the Constitution. The future of any present-day criminal suspect may depend on an argument about the intentions of men 200 years dead. It may equally depend on arguments about the extent to which the literal intentions of the men who wrote the Constitution should govern a country that, since those founding years, has ended slavery, expanded voting rights, multiplied its population and territory, acquired professional police forces, and absorbed thousands of inventions, including photography, telephones, wiretaps, automobiles, speed traps, air travel, cocaine, automatic weapons, urine tests, fingerprinting, DNA typing, psychiatry, and the Internet.

Learning what the Bill of Rights meant at its ratification in 1791, together with its various meanings over the years since then, can be important to modern constitutional interpretation. A further step back into the history of the English legal system and its application to the North American east coast through colonial governments in the seventeenth and eighteenth centuries, when much of the United States' legal system was created, can also help.

There is not much space here to discuss history, as this book is dedicated to current controversies, but present-day arguments can frequently be reinforced by citing similar situations in the past or by using historical background to explain how we got where we are today. Supreme Court justices frequently consider what the Founding Fathers might have thought of a present-day situation, and scholarly debate about the Fourth Amendment in particular has taken a strong turn into the realm of historical interpretation. There is a continuing dispute among legal historians about whether the framers of the Constitution, who lived before full-time professional police forces were invented, thought that there should be any such thing as a search without a warrant—although today, fewer searches are conducted with warrants than without.[2]

English legal history is one of the strongest influences on the present-day U.S. system. The idea that ordinary people have legal rights owes a lot to medieval notions of "English liberty" and particularly to King John's Magna Carta agreement of 1215, which first established that a law could be more important than the king.[3] Ideas about the legal rights of unpopular or powerless people developed further in England and its American colonies during the seventeenth and eighteenth centuries under the influence of political and religious conflicts. The debates of those days are still cited in present-day law. The famous 1966 case of *Miranda* v. *Arizona*, which says that police must remind arrested people of their right to remain silent and their right to consult a lawyer, refers back to the trial of a political activist named John Lilburn in England in 1637. The Lilburn case persuaded England's Parliament to ban the notorious Star Chamber practice of forcing suspects to testify against themselves. Likewise, *Miranda* banned the twentieth-century practice of questioning ignorant criminal suspects without telling them that they could refuse to answer.[4] The Fourth Amendment derives almost directly from disputes over political pamphlet seizures in England in the 1760s, especially in the case of *Wilkes v. Wood*, and indiscriminate searches of merchants' buildings by customs tax officials in colonial Massachusetts, which were challenged in the 1761 Writs of Assistance case.[5]

- **Should arguments about something that happened in 1761 affect the freedom of present-day criminal suspects?**

The United States Constitution spelled out an idea that had been less clearly implied in English law: The people are always entitled to certain fundamental rights that no person or group in government may violate, either by abuse of power individually or by making unjust laws. The Fourth Amendment and the rest of the Bill of Rights had little to do with the actual treatment of criminal suspects for many years. Throughout the nineteenth century and well into the twentieth, search and seizure practices developed without close constitutional scrutiny. During this time, professional U.S. police forces replaced less organized groups of watchmen and developed basic methods and institutional cultures. This is not to say that officers in these forces failed to serve justice, but rather to suggest that they at first handled suspects less formally, under fewer written rules, and with much more practical authority to make arrests and much less risk of having their decisions reversed in court.[6] It has, however, been argued that some police departments' institutional cultures were influenced by the explicitly racist tradition of "slave patrols," which were groups of white property owners, required to serve by local law, who searched roads and slave quarters at night to discourage rebellion or escape.[7]

A big step toward the application of the Bill of Rights to everyday law enforcement happened with the passage of the Fourteenth Amendment as part of a group of post–Civil War laws and constitutional amendments intended to mend the country and confirm the citizenship rights of former slaves. Its key Section I provides:

> All persons born or naturalized in the United States, and subject to the jurisdiction thereof, are citizens of the United States and of the State wherein they reside. No State shall make or enforce any law which shall abridge the privileges or immunities of citizens of the United States; nor shall any State deprive any person of life, liberty, or property, without due process of law; nor deny to any person within its jurisdiction the equal protection of the laws.[8]

The "due process" and "equal protection" clauses of the Fourteenth Amendment became important conduits that the Supreme Court used to give practical local effect to the Bill of Rights. This transition started slowly. Only scattered Fourteenth Amendment rights decisions—such as *Yick Wo* v. *Hopkins*— which established that the Fourteenth Amendment entitled "all persons" in the United States regardless of their immigration or citizenship status, to "due process of law" and the "equal protection of the laws,"[9] appeared in the nineteenth century. (This amendment, however, does not give precisely equal rights to all noncitizens—they have fewer rights as their ties to the United States decrease.[10])

In criminal law, a few isolated cases began a slow process of Supreme Court reasoning that led up to a radically new conclusion: that the Bill of Rights, first viewed as a restraint on the powers of the federal government, ought to affect the behavior of local police in everyday situations.[11] Important landmarks in this process included the famous "Scottsboro Boys" case, in which the Supreme Court found that a group of poorly educated young black men had been convicted of rape without a fair chance to present an effective defense.[12]

In the 1960s, the famous Warren Court began to apply criminal procedure protections in the Bill of Rights to people under arrest or investigation by local police. The result was a jolting collision between long-standing police practices and the newly interpreted language of the Constitution.

For the Fourth Amendment, the turning point came in 1961, when the Supreme Court, then in its active years under Chief Justice Warren, ruled in the illegal-search case of *Mapp* v. *Ohio* that the exclusionary rule applies to local police searches. This rule, first applied to federal law enforcement in the 1914 case of *Weeks* v. *United States*, requires that evidence obtained by illegal search must be thrown out of court ("suppressed").[13] Other key Warren Court decisions that protected the rights of criminal defendants (people on trial for crimes) included *Gideon* v. *Wainwright*, which solidly established the right of poor people charged with crimes to free legal representation,[14] and *Miranda* v. *Arizona*,[15] which requires police to deliver the famous warning that advises suspects of the right to remain silent under police questioning and to consult an attorney.

The Warren Court continued to establish many more protections for suspects' rights during their arrest, questioning, detention, and trial. In reaching these and other decisions, the Court slowly gave majority approval to the doctrine of selective incorporation, which holds that parts of the Bill of Rights are "incorporated" in the Due Process Clause of the Fourteenth Amendment and therefore apply to "state action"—which, as now understood, means the behavior of both state and local officials. With respect to criminal procedure, the Court essentially found that people being arrested or tried by state or local officials were entitled to most protections of the Fourth, Fifth,

Sixth and Eighth Amendments—the right against unreasonable search and seizure; the right to refuse to be a witness against oneself; the rights to a "speedy and public" trial by jury, with the right to call one's own witnesses and confront one's accusers, and to have a lawyer; and finally, the right to be free of "cruel and unusual punishment."

Search and seizure law also went through a modernization process in the twentieth century, most notably under the influence of Prohibition. This national ban on alcoholic beverages, which lasted from 1920 through 1933, increased both organized crime and official searching for contraband. Around the same time, the automobile and the telephone were becoming widely available; Prohibition gangsters began to use them in new ways that the law had to adapt to handle.[16]

Two important search and seizure cases related directly to Prohibition were *Carroll* v. *U.S.* and *Olmstead* v. *U.S.* The *Carroll* case, which is still on the books and cited as precedent, found that police who stopped a known bootlegger's car on general suspicion did not need a warrant to search the vehicle. (The car did in fact have 69 quarts of bootleg whiskey in its upholstery.)

FROM THE BENCH

Justice Brandeis, dissenting in *Olmstead* v. *U.S.*, 1928

It is, of course, immaterial where the physical connection with the telephone wires leading into the defendants' premises was made. And it is also immaterial that the intrusion was in aid of law enforcement. Experience should teach us to be most on our guard to protect liberty when the government's purposes are beneficent. Men born to freedom are naturally alert to repel invasion of their liberty by evil-minded rulers. The greatest dangers to liberty lurk in insidious encroachment by men of zeal, well-meaning but without understanding . . .

Source: *Olmstead* v. *U.S.*, 277 U.S. 438 (1928)

The *Olmstead* case is no longer in effect and is interesting as an example of the legal distortions that sometimes develop from conflicting views of a new technology—as, in the present day, officials and legislators have varying ideas about Internet privacy. This case concerned a federal bust of a massive Seattle bootlegging operation that had been illegally selling up to 200 cases of Canadian liquor per day. Acting without a warrant, federal agents tapped four telephone lines that the operation used to discuss not only liquor sales, but also, apparently, Olmstead's corrupt dealings with Seattle police. The eavesdropping led to more than 72 indictments. (Under the Fifth Amendment, federal prosecutions for serious offenses can be brought only after grand jury indictment.) The Court majority arrived at a decision that may now seem absurd: that, because the agents who tapped Olmstead's phone lines had not physically entered his property, they had not violated his Fourth Amendment rights. In dissent from the majority opinion, Justice Louis D. Brandeis wrote a famous protest about the Bill of Rights as protector of "the right to be let alone—the most comprehensive of rights and the right most valued by civilized men."

Much later—after the official political eavesdropping of the McCarthy 1950s, among other things—Justice Brandeis's view was endorsed by *Katz* v. *U.S.*[17] The present rule is defined by *Katz*: "the Fourth Amendment protects people, not places." In the *Katz* case in particular, the Supreme Court found that the defendant, in placing a call from a phone booth, had a "reasonable expectation of privacy" and law enforcement officials were bound to honor it. This did not mean that police were flatly barred from eavesdropping on Katz's calls, but it did mean that the eavesdropping would have been legal only if a magistrate had first issued a search warrant based on probable cause to suspect Katz of specific crimes.

Katz's importance for wiretapping has since been eclipsed by federal legislation.[18] However, this case remains important in other constitutional criminal law for its broader rule that people have Fourth Amendment rights no matter where they are—at home, in a phone booth, or walking down the street.

As with most Supreme Court criminal law decisions, the *Mapp, Gideon, Miranda,* and *Katz* rulings were based on appeals brought by people who had been convicted of crimes in local trial courts. The decisions in their favor were not storybook victories of good over evil. Instead, they illustrated the more complex notion that a person who is very possibly guilty of a crime can also be a victim of injustice.

Clarence Gideon was eventually cleared of his crime—the story is told by Anthony Lewis's classic book *Gideon's Trumpet*[19] and in the 1980 film of the same name. On the other hand, the police who searched Dollree Mapp's house really did find pornography, Ernesto Miranda did confess to kidnapping and rape, and Katz was phoning in illegal gambling bets.[20] Yet in all those cases the Court ruled that, because the police did not play fair, the defendant should go free.

Mapp and *Katz* worked on the principle of a uniform Fourth Amendment "exclusionary rule," meaning that if a search violated a defendant's rights, any evidence it produced could not be considered at trial. In practice, this meant that if the police did not play fair, even a guilty defendant should go free—a decision that has upsetting consequences, although it does enforce good police behavior by appealing to police officers' desire to keep criminals behind bars. *Mapp* and *Katz* (along with many other cases) established the exclusionary rule for violations of Fourth Amendment search and seizure rights. *Miranda* had a similar effect with respect to the Fifth Amendment right against self-incrimination: It held that, if a confession was unconstitutionally obtained, the results cannot be considered in court.

The Warren Court is stereotyped as liberal, but another great 1960s landmark case is part of the story, and this one favors police and prosecutors, not defendants: the 1968 case of *Terry* v. *Ohio*.[21] An experienced Cleveland police detective named McFadden spotted three men who seemed strangely interested in a particular store window. He suspected that they were "casing a job"—planning to rob the store. In a few moments of brave police work, he confronted the men by himself, managed to frisk them all for weapons by patting their clothing, and took away guns that his pat search discovered in two of the men's pockets.

The Supreme Court decided that this search and seizure was proper, and it announced one of the most important rules in criminal law: An officer who has a "reasonable suspicion" of criminal behavior in a street situation that does not allow time to obtain a search warrant may conduct an "investigatory stop" of a suspect. If an officer making this kind of stop reasonably fears that the suspect may be armed, the officer may frisk or "pat search" the suspect for weapons and may seize as evidence any weapons found in this way.

An arrest is only proper if police believe that, "more likely than not," the suspect has committed the alleged offense, but a *Terry* stop is all right even if there is less than an even chance that the suspect has done something wrong.[22] Today, *Terry* stops are an important daily part of police patrol work—frequently with no record created. A skilled officer can make a *Terry* stop so casually that the suspect doesn't realize a process that has formal rules and extremely important consequences has begun.

Now, 40 years after *Mapp* v. *Ohio*, courts have softened the Warren Court's strict limits on police practice. As the War on Terrorism empowers police agencies in the name of protecting against catastrophic threats, the debate over police powers and practices has intensified. The main present-day arguments about the Fourth Amendment involve defining the circumstances when a police officer may "reasonably" search a person, car, bag, or building without specific official permission and when the officer has to leave the suspect alone until—or unless—a judge issues a warrant to allow the search.

The Fourth Amendment, in general, still stands for the idea that the police may not search people or break into their houses for unjust reasons or for no reason at all. The basic rule is that people are to be left alone. Searches and seizures are allowed only as exceptions to that rule. People do not automatically have to explain themselves to the government. If it bothers individuals, the government owes them and the public an explanation. What happens in practice is, of course, another matter. Often, it has more to do with police traditions developed in the days before the Warren Court brought the rights of suspects to center stage. For the past 20 years and more, courts have been receptive to arguments that the Warren Court due process precedents restrain police behavior too harshly. The courts have now moved some distance in the opposite direction.

With the 2001 inauguration of the U.S. War on Terrorism, further permissions were granted to police forces and investigative agencies. Debate over the search and seizure issues consequently has sharpened over the past years. The whole search and seizure debate is too intricate to summarize entirely in this book, but the chapters that follow present some basic pro and con points on the legal scope of police powers, the police and security practice of profiling, and the extent to which police conduct conforms to the requirements of a democratic society.

Summary

This book considers "search and seizure" as broadly understood in the United States under the Fourth Amendment and other laws. It concerns the early stages of the criminal justice process, from initial police suspicion to the arrest and charging decisions. It is not a manual for those facing criminal charges or other legal trouble, but an aid to discussion.

The laws of the United States that affect suspects' rights have a history derived in large part from older English law and disputes that arose shortly before the American Revolution. Important ideas that derive from this history are that certain rights outweigh any individual's authority and that government has to justify any intrusion on people's rights. Major twentieth-century changes in the law of search and seizure included the Supreme Court's slow arrival at the notion that the Fourteenth Amendment applied the Bill of Rights to restrain the behavior of state and local officials and decisions made during Prohibition to keep up with expanding crime and new technology. The "due process revolution" of the 1960s expanded many rights for criminal suspects, notably in the cases of *Mapp*, *Gideon*, *Miranda*, and *Katz*, but in *Terry* the same Warren Court granted the traditional power of police officers to detain people for brief investigation without evidence of any crime committed. Since the 1960s, the trend has been toward greater powers for police and prosecutors—a pattern that has intensified since the September 2001 terrorist attacks.

"Technicalities" in Criminal Trials Protect Everybody's Freedoms

W hen the police came to visit Dollree Mapp one day in 1957, they were investigating a bombing of the home of Don King—the same Don King who later became a famous boxing promoter. The officers believed that King, Mapp, and the chief suspect in the attack were involved in illegal gambling, and they saw a car in Mapp's driveway that belonged to another reputed gambler who might help them find the suspect. In fact, the car's owner was not in Mapp's house. When the police knocked, Mapp called her lawyer, who advised her not to open the door unless they had a search warrant. The police broke in. When they showed a paper that they claimed was a warrant, she grabbed it. They wrestled it back. (It was not a real warrant, only an affidavit.) The police also twisted her hand, handcuffed her, and tore up the entire duplex where she lived, searching for anything illegal whatsoever. Their "fishing expedition" did find an excuse for arresting her: The conviction that she eventually appealed to the Supreme Court was based on some dirty books and a rude doodle, partly found in the basement, which she said had been left by a former tenant.[23]

Dollree Mapp does not sound like an especially solid citizen —but since when is being a nonsolid citizen a crime punishable by invasion of one's home by the police? The true motives of the officers who turned her house upside down cannot be known, but it is possible to guess that they meant to "punish" her for insisting on her rights and refusing to open the door. What if Mapp's two-to-seven-year prison term for obscenity had been allowed to stand, despite a finding that the search was a violation of her rights? Would the officers then have learned a lesson about respecting people's rights? If Mapp's home was searched with impunity one day, would anything but tidier personal reputations prevent other people's homes from being searched similarly? Is the rule of law operating properly when it is personal reputation, not law, that protects a person from being mistreated?

When the "exclusionary rule" weakens, so do everyone's rights.

The constitutional amendments that protect an individual from government intrusion tend to be under-respected because unpopular people are the most likely to assert them. The Fourth Amendment, especially, is discussed most often in criminal courtrooms where a defendant is trying to beat a criminal charge by arguing that some piece of evidence that tends to prove a crime, for example, a bag of drugs found in a car, should be thrown out of court because it was seized in an unconstitutional search. This kind of company makes the Fourth Amendment itself sound like something vaguely criminal—a sneaky excuse used by shifty people who always have something to hide. From another point of view, the Fourth Amendment has great dignity: It is one of the main differences between a democratic society, in which the government must justify its conduct to its citizens, and a police state, in which the government demands justifications from individuals but gives none in return.

Civil libertarians and criminal defense attorneys value the exclusionary rule and lament that, in the decades since the 1960s, it has been punched full of holes by court decisions favoring the cops' side of too many stories. (The exclusionary rule is principally understood as the rule announced in the Supreme Court case of *Mapp* v. *Ohio* that, if the police violated the Fourth Amendment rights of a person on trial for a crime, the evidence they obtained through that violation cannot be used against that defendant in court. Exclusionary rules are also said to exist for the Fifth Amendment right against self-incrimination under *Miranda* v. *Arizona*, the Sixth Amendment right to legal counsel, and the Fourteenth Amendment right to due process of law. When people say "*the* exclusionary rule," however, the reference is generally to the Fourth Amendment rule on search and seizure.)

Sometimes, as in *Mapp*, the exclusionary rule forces the criminal justice system to let go of someone who probably did break the law. Yet every day judges and lawyers in the criminal justice system, who are themselves sworn to uphold the laws, also uphold the exclusionary rule for a number of compelling reasons.

First, the exclusionary rule itself is the law of the land, as stated through Supreme Court decisions that override all other law in the United States and as interpreted nationwide by decisions in every state and federal court that handles criminal matters. After his retirement from the Supreme Court, Justice Potter Stewart argued that people who don't like the exclusionary rule should complain not to the Supreme Court, but to the Framers who wrote the Constitution. He argued, as many others do, that the incomplete enforcement of laws is simply the price we pay for having a Fourth Amendment. This same argument— that the United States chose long ago to give up some safety in return for more freedom—can be extended to all the Bill of Rights provisions that keep official hands off of individual rights. Citizens' rights sometimes get in the way of the police or other authorities, and when that happens, it is not a defect in the system. It is an example of the Constitution doing its job, which is to preserve a balance of power between the individual and the state.

Second, and possibly more important, the exclusionary rule is one of the best tools available to make the police obey the law. It does not help simply to tell an officer to respect people's rights or even to make it a crime for members of a police force to mistreat suspects. On one hand, an order to respect rights has to be enforceable or it will simply be shrugged off as well-meaning but impractical advice. On the other hand, police officers are trusted as protectors of the public and it is not easy for prosecutors, police executives, or, for that matter, the general public, to turn around and accuse them of crimes, so that is not likely to happen except in drastic cases such as the famous 1991 Rodney King beating in Los Angeles. Furthermore, police forces could not function if an officer had to be put on trial every time a suspect made a claim about a rights violation. There must be some mechanism that gives importance to suspects' claims about rights violations and yet does not turn the arresting officer into the accused party every time such an issue goes to court.

Retired Supreme Court Justice Potter Stewart, writing about the *Mapp* exclusionary rule

Much of the criticism leveled at the exclusionary rule is misdirected; it is more properly directed at the Fourth Amendment itself.... The inevitable result of the Constitution's prohibition against unreasonable searches and seizures and its requirement that no warrant shall issue but upon probable cause is that police officers who obey its strictures will catch fewer criminals. That is not a political outcome impressed upon an unwilling citizenry by unbeknighted judges. It is the price the framers anticipated and were willing to pay to ensure the sanctity of the person, the home, and property against unrestrained governmental power....

Source: Stewart, "The Road to *Mapp* v. *Ohio,*" pp. 1392–1393.

The exclusionary rule turns respect for constitutional rights into a goal of the law enforcement profession, in a much more practical way than any number of nice words could achieve. Police officers on patrol know that they will not be able to put a suspect behind bars unless they can present cleanly acquired evidence that a judge will allow to be considered at trial—that is, they cannot give the judge any reason to "suppress" the evidence under the exclusionary rule. Police supervisors therefore have reason to remind their officers not to commit rights violations that will cause cases to be thrown out of court. Prosecutors, meanwhile, often decide to let an arrested person go free without bringing charges in court because the suspect's rights clearly were violated and there is no point wasting time to begin prosecution that would be defeated by a successful motion to suppress.

In other words, the exclusionary rule, at least in theory, exists to make sure that criminal convictions are obtained cleanly or not at all. In practice, the exclusionary rule has been weakened and there are some kinds of civil rights violations that it never did have the power to stop. The exclusionary rule does have a significant effect, however, and although it is costly in terms of lost convictions, it is a respected safeguard in American criminal justice.

There are, of course, ways other than the exclusionary rule to restrain lawless or bullying police behavior. One method is to remove procedural barriers to civil rights lawsuits—though, if anything, the barriers have risen more than fallen in recent years. Courts can also issue orders that require certain conduct ("injunctive relief") or they can impose fines on police departments, jails, and prosecutors. Prosecutors can bring criminal charges against officers themselves in exceptional cases. More generally, courts have power to declare laws unconstitutional, with the Supreme Court having the last word on that question, and courts have used this power to invalidate laws that invited or required certain kinds of discrimination. The courts have also struck down a number of vague laws that police used to create charges against people they regarded as troublemakers who were not doing anything specifically prohibited. The Supreme Court of the early 1970s found it unconstitutional for police to arrest people for vaguely undesirable statuses such as "being a disorderly person."[24]

These other approaches to the regulation of police conduct are discussed later in this book. The remainder of this chapter considers the extent to which the exclusionary rule actually does (or doesn't) protect the public from official intrusions.

The rights of the accused have been cut back dangerously.

Police conduct expert Jerome Skolnick wrote, "Despite far more deference to law enforcement than is commonly understood to be the case, the 1960s were unquestionably the pinnacle of constitutional reform in procedural law, setting higher standards for lawful police conduct than cops had ever faced."[25] Those new, higher standards provoked a backlash that was still in progress as of this writing. In 1975, law professor Francis Allen commented from the perspective of an indignant liberal:

> In the presidential campaign of 1968 the bewildering problems of crime in the United States were represented simply as a war between the "peace forces" and the "criminal forces." The decision in *Miranda* evoked a chorus of criticism of the [Supreme] Court, ranging from the excited to the psychotic. Congress responded with the Omnibus Crime Control and Safe Streets Act of 1968, some provisions of which were obviously retaliatory. These events combined to create an atmosphere that, to say the least, was unfavorable to the continued vitality of the Warren Court's mission in criminal cases.[26]

Allen noted, with a hint of understatement, that "fears of crime and of the collapse of public order are a powerful political dynamic in American society, a perception that appears to have sometimes eluded practitioners of liberal politics." [27] The Court has issued decisions of widely varied effect since Chief Justice Warren's 1969 retirement, but in the area of criminal procedure it has backed away steadily from the "activist" decisions of the 1960s.

A glance through the cases cited in this book will show how often drug enforcement in particular has led to court decisions that expanded police search and seizure powers. A law professor writing in 1987 suggested that the courts were developing an informal "drug exception to the Bill of Rights," and that "what Laurence Tribe described as the Constitution's 'pivotal, even mythological place in our national consciousness' is rapidly being eroded by a positivist, bureaucratic attitude that we can—must—do whatever is deemed necessary or expedient in waging the War on Drugs." [28]

Like other rights of the accused, the exclusionary rule has been whittled down in recent years. There are now many court-made exceptions to the rule. Generally, the rationale for such exceptions is that the exclusionary rule exists to keep the system honest, not to help individual suspects—and, as long as the rule in general applies solidly enough to make police and prosecutors obey the Constitution, it should not have to apply in certain specific cases.

Civil libertarians and defense lawyers, however, worry, for example, about decisions in which an officer's "good faith" is the excuse for not applying the exclusionary rule. Can an officer who wants a conviction badly enough really be trusted when he says that, honest, he didn't mean to violate any rights?

The Supreme Court has continued to use the exclusionary rule to limit searches and seizures. Under *Katz*, people have a Fourth Amendment expectation of privacy no matter where they go. Fourth Amendment constitutional case law is designed only to stop the police from acting impulsively or without sufficient evidence, however; it does not block searches or arrests that are based on probable cause. The definition of the phrase "probable cause" originates in the Fourth Amendment text itself and is continually disputed, in ever finer shades of meaning, in courtrooms all over the United States. Furthermore, *Terry* v. *Ohio*[29] allows police to stop and question people on the street without probable cause as long as they can point to specific facts that led them to suspect wrongdoing. Under *Terry*, officers may frisk people stopped in this manner for weapons if it seems necessary to protect the officers' safety. The frisk, in turn, can lead to further investigation—for example, if the officer, while "checking for weapons," feels a shape in a person's pocket that might be drug paraphernalia.

In public, police can make a warrantless arrest of anyone who commits a crime in front of them. They can also make a warrantless arrest in public of a person who they have "reasonable grounds" to believe has committed a felony anywhere. ("Reasonable grounds" is similar to probable cause.[30]) Wherever they are, police officers can act on anything they can see "in plain view."

Definitions of "expectation of privacy" and "plain view" have had to keep pace with the many methods officers have developed to learn more about suspects when they have no probable cause to make a search. Courts have found that discoveries were made through plain view, not searches, when officers used their unaided senses of sight, hearing, and smell and also when they have used drug-sniffing dogs, flashlights, binoculars, and hovering helicopters. Use of sophisticated equipment like heat sensors counts as a search, but poking through suspects' garbage does not, based on the reasoning that people have no expectation of privacy in garbage they have voluntarily set out for collection.[31]

Courts have increasingly favored prosecutors on the meaning of "consent" to a police entry or search. Generally speaking, if the police ask for permission to enter a home to search places or items such as a car or luggage, a person who agrees—even when the request sounds like an order—is said to have "consented" and thereby given up ("waived") Fourth Amendment search and seizure rights that would otherwise apply.[32] Warrantless entry to a home is permissible when police are allowed in by a relative or roommate who has "common authority over the premises" with the suspect.[33] Consent to an official search can also be forced on people for reasons other than police authority; for example, families on aid can be required to accept home inspections as a condition for receiving welfare benefits.[34] In addition, state laws may require that people convicted of crimes who are living on parole or probation must accept all police searches of themselves and their homes, even for no reason, until the parole or probation expires.

People who are not subject to any special restriction and who assert their right to refuse consent for a search do have some protections against search and seizure, especially when they are at home. This is true provided they live in conventional homes like houses or apartments as opposed to a movable trailer, for example, which qualifies as a vehicle.[35]

Officers generally may not enter a house or apartment to make a search or arrest without a resident's permission unless they have a warrant.[36] Officers may enter immediately in a few narrowly defined "exigent circumstances"—emergencies, more or less. Among these are the need to prevent suspects from destroying evidence and the "hot pursuit" of a suspect who escapes into a building. Exigent circumstances do not justify entry into a home unless police also have probable cause to believe that they will find the perpetrator or evidence of a crime.[37]

Generally, a magistrate may issue an arrest warrant or search warrant only on finding that there is probable cause to believe that a specific person has committed a crime or that evidence of a specific crime will be found in the location to be searched. A warrant for the arrest of a particular person does not authorize police to enter someone else's home in search of that person.[38] Police who arrested a man with a warrant at his own home were entitled to search the arrestee and the area directly around him as a "search incident to a lawful arrest," but they could not automatically search his entire house.[39] A warrant to search 1 of 20 apartments in a building did not allow an additional search of the basement.[40]

On the other hand, a search warrant can authorize a thorough search of an entire large property such as a ranch.[41] Also, police looking for things described in a warrant may pay attention to other items "in plain view" in a house and may seize them if there is probable cause to think that the items are evidence of a crime. According to the 1990 case *Horton* v. *California*, it is acceptable for an officer to obtain a search warrant for one thing as an excuse, or "pretext," to enter an area where the officer hopes a more important piece of evidence will be in plain view.[42]

For areas other than the home, there are fine degrees of distinction among levels of expectation of privacy. Special rules cover "open fields" on private property, "curtilage" (the semiprivate yard area around a house), private and public areas of businesses, and yards or parking lots around business buildings.[43]

There is no obligation to open the door to police who have no warrant. Police may assert the right to enter under one of the emergency exceptions, and if they choose to enter physically, anyone trying to stop them physically could face charges of interfering with an officer, resisting arrest, and worse. It is a difficult question when a suspect who does open the front door to a house may be pursued inside. In 1976, the Supreme Court approved warrantless entry when a woman suspected of drug dealing opened the door, stood right on the threshold, saw the police, and backed into the house, leaving the door open.[44] In contrast, the New Hampshire case of *State* v. *Morse* found that police improperly made a warrantless entry to a motel room after a rape suspect opened his door but did not step out.[45] The status of a person who stands right in a doorway is in dispute.[46]

There are a number of special situations and institutions for which search and seizure rights are reduced. Among these are schools, for which the Supreme Court has held that public school officials have to respect Fourth Amendment rights because they are government representatives just as police are—but because of the special need to maintain order in schools, school officials can search students without a warrant or probable cause as long as the search is "reasonable."[47]

Vehicle searches belong to their own special category. Fourth Amendment protections are fewer for vehicles than for homes, but officers do not have an automatic right to search a vehicle. Officers are allowed to look into a car from outside and to act further on the basis of anything suspicious they see, hear, or smell because of the plain view rule. The driver of a moving vehicle that has been stopped will probably be required under state law, as a condition of the driving privilege, to show certain documents, such as driver's license, car registration, and insurance, on demand. The driver and other occupants do *not* have to consent to a search. Without consent, an officer may only search an automobile under carefully defined circumstances—mainly when there is probable cause to believe that it contains evidence of illegal activity.[48] The circumstances that allow a search keep expanding, however, to the point that an intelligent officer who wants to search a car can usually find a rationale for doing so. When police arrest someone from a car, they may search the car's passenger compartment.[49]

The *Carroll* bootlegger case opened the door for a continuing series of precedents that now let police stop and search an entire vehicle without a warrant if it is "readily mobile" and they have probable cause to think that it contains contraband such as drugs.[50] Containers within cars are somewhat more protected, but if there is probable cause to search the whole car, containers within the car may also be searched.[51]

Police permission to search cars and other places legally may build from one kind of warrantless search authority to another, resulting in a combined effect that leaves the subjects of the investigation essentially without rights against search. This happened in the case of *Wyoming* v. *Houghton*. The decision said that Wyoming Highway Patrol officers acted correctly in a stop and search that followed at least three separate stages, each justifying the next. Officers first stopped a car carrying three people for "speeding and driving with a faulty brake light." Then an officer saw a syringe in "plain view" in the driver's shirt pocket. He asked about the syringe; the driver admitted using it for drugs. Because the driver made this admission, the officers had reason under 1990s search precedents to search for drugs in the passenger compartment of the car. They also looked in a passenger's purse, where they learned from an identity card that she had given a false name; they kept searching and found that the purse contained drugs. This passenger, Sandra Houghton, was convicted on felony drug charges. The question to the Supreme Court was whether the officers should have opened Houghton's purse and searched the containers inside it, because she was not the driver. The Court found that, in looking for drugs, the officers were justified in searching any of passengers' belongings "that are capable of concealing the object of the search."[52]

If police are entitled to tow a vehicle—even, for example, under a local parking ordinance—they are allowed to "inventory" the vehicle's contents, which can mean a full warrantless search. If they find drugs or other evidence of crime in the vehicle during the inventory, the evidence can be introduced against the owner in court.[53]

A somewhat different kind of seizure involves the taking of property not as evidence, but as asset forfeiture under state and federal laws. There are many forfeiture laws, of which the best known are probably the federal drug asset forfeiture laws. The forfeiture provisions at 21 U.S. Code § 881 allow federal authorities to take, on a showing of probable cause only, items including real estate, vehicles, or money used in the drug trade. Section 853 allows similar forfeiture of assets of people who have been convicted on drug charges. People whose property has been taken are entitled under Fifth and Fourteenth amendment due process rights to challenge the taking, although there have been complaints about the fairness of the procedures available for such challenges.

Under a state forfeiture statute, in *Florida* v. *White*,[54] the Supreme Court allowed state officials to take away and keep a car that had been used to carry drugs two months earlier. These seizures are not very effectively limited by Fourth Amendment law, nor by the Fifth Amendment, which ordinarily prohibits the taking of private property without just compensation. The Supreme Court has at least held that a civil forfeiture following from a criminal conviction is a kind of punishment and can therefore be restrained by the Excessive Fines Clause of the Eighth Amendment,[55] but this finding is overshadowed by a later decision that said that civil forfeitures do not count as punishment for purposes of the Fifth Amendment's Double Jeopardy Clause.[56]

Forfeiture statutes are intensely controversial, especially when households have lost livelihoods and when items have been taken before any crime was proven in court.[57] Part of the purpose of forfeiture is to prevent high-level criminals from using ill-gotten gains to pay lavishly for their own criminal defense, but some defendants have complained that, after the government took their money and property, they could not pay a lawyer at all.[58] Defendants are entitled to free legal representation in criminal cases if they cannot afford to pay their own lawyers, but there is no right to free legal help to contest a civil forfeiture.

Some of the saddest stories come from people whose property was taken because they used marijuana to relieve illness. One well-known case was that of Robert Brewer, a retired postal service employee with terminal cancer who was caught with eight marijuana plants under a grow light and half a pound of the drug at his Idaho home. He and his wife owned a van that allowed him to ease his pain and swelling by lying down during the 270-mile drives to Salt Lake City for treatment. The van was seized under a drug statute, so the Brewers had to make the drive by car. This story and several others appeared in "Presumed Guilty," a condemnatory series in the *Pittsburgh Press* newspaper in 1991.[59] A Justice Department reply at the time had several criticisms of the series, including that it failed to make clear that innocent property owners could challenge the seizures. The reply disputed aspects of some stories, although not the Brewers' story.[60] The series reflects conditions as of many years ago, but it is still circulated on Websites critical of the War on Drugs.

Miranda has been weakened, also at the expense of the public.

Like *Mapp* v. *Ohio* and the Fourth Amendment, the famous *Miranda* v. *Arizona* Fifth Amendment case was decided as a rule to keep the system honest, not necessarily to help individual defendants. Ernesto Miranda had clearly confessed to kidnapping and rape, and the court opinion does not sound especially sorry for him as a person. Chief Justice Warren, a former prosecutor, wrote the decision. In establishing the now-familiar Miranda warning, he said that it was a needed protection for the Fifth Amendment right against being compelled to testify against oneself. He noted that physical torture was no longer common in U.S. police stations, but he also wrote that standard police techniques included psychological methods that were highly effective in getting confessions, especially with suspects like Miranda, who was poorly educated and mentally ill, and another man in the same case who had dropped out of sixth grade.

The exact words of the *Miranda* warning may vary, but the decision requires that a person who is questioned in custody— that is, while under police control and not free to go—must be told of the right to remain silent, of the fact that "anything said can and will be used against the individual in court," of the right to have a lawyer and to have the lawyer present during questioning, and of the right to have a lawyer appointed if the person cannot afford one.

> If the individual indicates in any manner, at any time prior to or during questioning, that he wishes to remain silent, the interrogation must cease. . . . If the individual states that he wants an attorney, the interrogation must cease until an attorney is present. At that time, the individual must have an opportunity to confer with the attorney and to have him present during any subsequent questioning. If the individual cannot obtain an attorney and he indicates that he wants one before speaking to police, they must respect his decision to remain silent.[61]

Police officers do not have to give *Miranda* warnings to people they arrest without questioning or to people they approach and question on the street—or even, in some cases, to people they have stopped and are preparing to arrest.[62] Any responses in such situations are taken as "voluntary," even if the officers act as though they are entitled to answers, because legally speaking the questioned person did have the right not to answer. Furthermore, the Supreme Court has upheld a Nevada state law that requires people to identify themselves to police on demand even if they have done nothing wrong.[63]

Suspects who receive *Miranda* warnings are often persuaded to talk to police before they can seek a lawyer's advice—a decision that tends to make things difficult for them and, later, for their defense attorneys. *Miranda* may not have had much effect on confessions in the long run, although some claim that it has reduced the effectiveness of police departments.

In 2004, the Supreme Court issued four decisions with mixed effects on the Fifth Amendment right to remain silent and the Sixth Amendment right to counsel. *Fellers* v. *United States* found that a suspect who had already been indicted still could not be questioned without being told his rights. *Chavez* v. *Martinez* found that a man who was questioned while in pain from gunshot wounds could not claim a violation of his Fifth Amendment rights because he was never prosecuted. *Missouri*

v. *Seibert* involved an officer who talked a murder suspect into a confession and then issued *Miranda* warnings and got her to repeat the confession on tape. In this case, the majority of a split court found that this particular interrogation was too intentionally deceptive to be constitutional but also suggested that double questioning might be acceptable if not done with deceptive intentions. *United States* v. *Patane* echoed *Seibert* but with worse consequences for defendants. In *Patane*, a suspect interrupted the officer who was advising him of his rights, saying that he knew them already. He apparently did not, as he then told the officer where to find a pistol he was illegally keeping in his home and allowed the officer to go and seize it there. The Court found that Patane's words could not be used as evidence against him but that the gun was "the physical fruit of a voluntary statement" and could be admitted as evidence.[64]

Summary

The exclusionary rule is a costly but important protection for the rights of suspects, but this rule has been cut back sharply, as have many other protections for the accused that the Supreme Court issued under Chief Justice Earl Warren in the 1960s. At present, warrantless searches are relatively easily approved, especially if they involve vehicles, and the growth of civil asset forfeiture as a prosecution tactic has created a new category of government "seizures" that Fourth Amendment jurisprudence has failed to prevent. Under *Miranda* and the Fifth Amendment right against self-incrimination, the "right to remain silent" warning is still required, but it barely survived the 2003–2004 Supreme Court term.

Too Much Concern for Formal Rights Interferes With Crime Fighting

The sympathetic part of the *Miranda* story is that Miranda was a poor, schizophrenic ninth-grade dropout who probably did not know that he had any rights in a police interrogation room and most likely would have been easily intimidated. The less appealing side of the story is that he was "a seriously disturbed individual with pronounced sexual fantasies" and the crime to which he had confessed was the kidnapping and rape of an 18-year-old girl. The famous Supreme Court decision threw his confessions out of court, essentially setting him free. Justice John Marshall Harlan, who included these facts in his dissent from the *Miranda* opinion, complained:

> One is entitled to feel astonished that the Constitution can be read to produce this result. These confessions were obtained during brief, daytime questioning conducted by two officers

and unmarked by any of the traditional indicia of coercion. They assured a conviction for a brutal and unsettling crime, for which the police had and quite possibly could obtain little evidence other than the victim's identifications, evidence which is frequently unreliable. There was, in sum, a legitimate purpose, no perceptible unfairness, and certainly little risk of injustice in the interrogation. Yet the resulting confessions, and the responsible course of police practice they represent, are to be sacrificed to the Court's own finespun conception of fairness which I seriously doubt is shared by many thinking citizens in this country.[65]

Plenty of people since Justice Harlan have wondered if there is a better way to honor the Constitution than by letting rapists go free.

The "exclusionary rule" is not worth its social price.

One of the loudest enduring criminal justice debates concerns the injustice of letting a guilty criminal go free "on a technicality." The technicality in such cases often has to do with the exclusionary rule—especially the Fourth Amendment exclusionary rule set out in *Mapp*, but also the parallel rules set out in *Miranda* for the Fifth Amendment and in other cases for rights such as the Sixth Amendment right to legal counsel. What hurts is the notion that, if the police break one of the ever more complicated rules for treatment of suspects, a criminal caught red-handed can still get out of jail free.

The trouble for ordinary police officers on patrol is that they can never be certain a defense attorney will not come up with an objection that invalidates their work. Constitutional rights requirements began to control police work much more in the 1960s, but the decisions did not stop then. In fact, for the past four decades, courts at all levels have been tinkering with the exclusionary rule and other restraints on police conduct, so every day there are more rules about rights. The best-intentioned police officer may not have time to memorize them all. Also, knowing all the rules will not necessarily help that moment when a cornered suspect reaches for something at his belt. Most police officers have less legal training than lawyers, yet they are the ones who have to put the courts' hairsplitting distinctions into practical effect. (Some officers happen to be lawyers, but they are rarely the ones on patrol.)

The situation was especially confusing for police departments in the mid-1960s, when major new rules like *Mapp* were relatively new and hard to interpret. Speaking to New York City lawyers in 1966, Chief Justice Roger J. Traynor of the California Supreme Court described confusion and fury within police forces. He was speaking a year after the Watts Riots in Los Angeles and just weeks before the *Miranda* decision, with *Mapp* already in effect but the *Katz* decision on expectation of privacy still to come. Traynor said:

> We now confront a long interim of living with the present conglomeration of federal and state rules, a devil's brew that is brewing wildly. Moreover, we must somehow find rational ways of applying constitutional rules of Olympian tenor to varied and ever-changing local scenes, where even law enforcement officers range from the scrupulously lawful to the soddenly lawless. The best of them are likely to grow impatient with recurring messages that loom to them, rightly or wrongly, as outlandish. Nothing is more unnerving to those amid the flak on the front lines than to receive commands of constitutional force phrased in unmistakably unclear [sic] language. In their view the courts are throwing the books at them, books that strike them of a weight either confoundedly heavy enough to leave them lightheaded or confoundedly light enough to leave them heavy-hearted. It is difficult to determine the nature and extent of their wounds, but from the outcry there is no doubt about their pain and suffering.[66]

Whereas civil libertarians saw the Supreme Court rights decisions as keeping the system fair, an opposing view saw justice betrayed, with bland, self-righteous officials at desks letting criminals go free. The 1971 Clint Eastwood film *Dirty Harry* gave this perspective to its hero: Harry pursues a killer ruthlessly, bucking a system that, in the name of abstract rights, would let a psychopath escape punishment.[67]

Joseph Wambaugh's 1973 true-crime bestseller, *The Onion Field*, also made into a movie, expressed similar outrage over the real trial of Gregory Powell and Jimmy Smith. As Wambaugh told it, Powell and Smith were small-time criminals who, in 1963, kidnapped two Los Angeles policemen and murdered one. The surviving officer, Karl Hettinger, suffered a guilt-driven mental collapse over his failure to save his partner. The book told a story of grotesquely extended criminal proceedings that created what was then the longest court transcript in California history, at 45,000 pages. Both kidnappers received long prison terms but escaped the death penalty, in part because of a court decision that said that they had been interrogated without adequate warnings and safeguards. Wambaugh quoted the original police interrogator, Pierce Brooks, as complaining, "They criticized *me* for getting too much of the truth. For too many confessions. . . We're only here now to protect the court record, to say the right things so a higher court can't reverse the case. Nobody cares about the truth."[68]

Driven by these kinds of sentiments, police officers' organizations became more involved in politics beginning in the 1960s—a development that creates worries about the separation of powers for some civil libertarians. Police organizations now give influential endorsements of candidates for office, several former police officers have become mayors of cities, and spokesmen for groups such as police officers' labor unions are now heard putting forward a view of police work as dangerous, heroic, underappreciated, overregulated, and misunderstood by those who have not faced its pressures.[69]

Constitutional rights can be respected without cheating justice.

During the four decades since *Mapp* v. *Ohio*, scholarly and judicial minds have found various exceptions to the harsh trade-off that would punish police misconduct with the fresh injustice of dropping otherwise legitimate criminal prosecutions.

The Supreme Court cases of *U.S.* v. *Calandra* and *U.S.* v. *Leon* are important precedents that have been interpreted in courts for a generation. Both allow some evidence into court despite constitutional violations, on the theory that the *Mapp* exclusionary rule is not an essential Fourth Amendment right of the accused person but just one way among many of supervising police conduct. These two cases establish that, even if evidence has been excluded because of a rights violation, it can be brought back in to impeach (cast doubt on) the testimony of a defendant who makes statements in court that do not match the excluded evidence. *Calandra* allowed evidence collected without probable cause to be introduced to a grand jury; *Leon* admitted evidence to trial that was seized without probable cause but by officers acting in "good faith" under a properly issued search warrant.[70]

In another exception, known as the "independent source" doctrine, the Supreme Court has held that illegally seized evidence

FROM THE BENCH

Chief Justice Warren Burger, *Nix* v. *Williams*, 1984

[T]he interest of society in deterring unlawful police conduct and the public interest in having juries receive all probative evidence of a crime are properly balanced by putting the police in the same, not a worse, position that they would have been in if no police error or misconduct had occurred. . . . When the challenged evidence has an independent source, exclusion of such evidence would put the police in a worse position than they would have been in absent any error or violation.

Source: *Nix* v. *Williams*, 467 U.S. 431, 443 (1984).

need not be excluded if a prosecutor can show that the police would have found it anyway had they acted lawfully.[71]

Meanwhile, the Supreme Court and interpreting lower courts have scaled back the definition of what constitutes a Fourth Amendment violation, trimming what some regarded as excessive 1960s insistence on the formal constitutional rights of the accused. At this time, there are almost more exceptions than rules left in Fourth Amendment jurisprudence, and although the exclusionary rule is not actually dead, certain scholars and judges are at work on fresh legal doctrines to replace it. A leading figure in this area is Akhil Reed Amar, a Yale professor who has been cited favorably in a number of Supreme Court decisions, including some on Fourth Amendment issues by Justices Antonin Scalia and Clarence Thomas.[72]

In a radical and highly controversial 1994 article, Amar challenged fellow scholars with his opening sentence: "The Fourth Amendment today is an embarrassment." He stated that decades of court-approved exceptions had carved search and seizure rights into lacework: "The result is a vast jumble of judicial pronouncements that is not merely complex and contradictory, but often perverse. Criminals go free, while honest citizens are intruded upon in outrageous ways with little or no real remedy." Instead of going on to say that the exclusionary rule or the warrant requirement needed strengthening, he argued that it was possible to read the Fourth Amendment in a way that bypassed those requirements entirely, so that future search and seizure doctrine could be based solely on defining a "reasonable" warrantless search. He suggested that police officers' respect for the Constitution could be enforced by other means—for example, dropping some of the immunity protections that insulate police officers from lawsuits by victims of illegal searches and using the power of courts to impose penalties for misconduct, with the penalty money possibly paid into public education funds, without benefiting accused criminals as the exclusionary rule does.[73]

Although Amar's new Fourth Amendment vision has drawn praise from the most conservative voices on the Supreme Court, his views are strongly enough civil libertarian that they do not match traditional "law and order" arguments. For example, police officers can hardly be expected to like his suggestion for making it easier to get compensation for misconduct out of officers' personal savings.

Miranda has "handcuffed" the cops.

Amar's ideas have some conservative implications, but they are not necessarily meant to increase or restore power to the police. Conservative legal academic Paul Cassell, who became a federal judge in 2002, worked from a very different perspective in the 1990s. He argued that the Supreme Court's *Miranda* decision had by itself kept police departments from solving crimes at their former rate.

Cassell, who was then a University of Utah College of Law professor, worked with an economist, Richard Fowles, to prepare a 1998 statistical study, "Handcuffing the Cops? A Thirty-Year Perspective on Miranda's Harmful Effects on Law Enforcement." The article quoted Richard Nixon as saying in his 1968 presidential campaign "that *Miranda* 'had the effect of seriously ham stringing [sic] the peace forces in our society and strengthening the criminal forces.'" That is essentially what Cassell and Fowles set out to prove with statistics.

The study showed declines in clearance rates reported by police departments to the FBI since the 1960s. In police terminology, a crime is "cleared" when the officers consider it solved —for example, when an investigation ends in an arrest or a suspect under questioning admits to an unsolved crime. Clearance rate figures are debatable for many reasons, in particular because they reflect only police accusations, not court convictions. Cassell and Fowles's clearance rate figures can at least arguably be read to say that police have solved crimes less efficiently ever since the 1950s.

Graphs in the study show clearance rates declining from the early 1960s and then falling more sharply beginning in 1966, the year *Miranda* was decided. The article says that "this suggests that the decision prevented police from solving a substantial number of crimes." It reports drops in clearance rates for both "violent" and "property" crimes and for all individual categories of crime except murder, rape, and assault. Data were patchier for "confession rates"—the rates at which suspects admitted to crimes—but Cassell and Fowles estimated that they were formerly "probably somewhere around 55–60%." In three post-*Miranda* studies, however, rates that Cassell and Fowles considered to be comparable fell between 33 and 40.3 percent.[74]

A lot of aspects of life (the level of confidence in public authorities, for example) changed in the United States in the 1960s and 1970s and so did some of the ways in which statistics were kept. Although Cassell and Fowles report that many different kinds of analysis show lower clearance rates after *Miranda*, correlation does not imply causation—that is, two things happening at the same time does not mean that one caused the other. A professor who published an opposing view in the same law review issue argued, among other things, that most big legal changes take time to show statistically visible effects in real life.[75]

The graphs in the article do slope downward in a suggestive way, and the authors suggest that, even if *Miranda* itself has not decreased the ability of police to solve crimes, the Warren Court's decisions in general may have had such an effect. This is an understandable suggestion. For example, the 1963 *Gideon* v. *Wainwright* decision on poor defendants' right to counsel brought many more defense lawyers into the criminal courts, and that could have made police and prosecutors more careful about making accusations.

Turning to anecdotal evidence—what individual people thought and saw at the time—Cassell and Fowles found several studies from the 1960s and 1970s in which police detectives and other law enforcement workers personally thought that *Miranda* had lowered clearance rates. They added, "Concerns about *Miranda* continue to be expressed by law enforcement. As one experienced detective recently explained, 'Most police are not really crazy about *Miranda*. It always gives the criminal that extra incentive not to say anything.'"

Efforts to undo *Miranda* have existed almost since the decision appeared. The 1968 Omnibus Crime Control and Safe Streets Act was a landmark effort by Congress to reassert law and order in a year marked by political violence and widespread challenges to traditional authority. The 1968 act has had a number of enduring effects. Its Title III, as amended, still provides important authority over police wiretaps.[76] It set up a system of grants to local law enforcement agencies that could only be used in compliance with federal antidiscrimination rules.[77] In addition, the act's Title II enacted an attempt to legislatively "repeal" *Miranda*. The repeal provision at 18 U.S. Code § 3501 attempted to require that all "voluntary" confessions must be admitted as evidence in federal prosecutions. This rule contradicts *Miranda* because, although it tells the judge to consider whether the suspect received warnings about rights, it allows a confession to be found "voluntary" even if no warnings were given.

In *Dickerson* v. *U.S.*, the Supreme Court upheld *Miranda* against § 3501, over a strong dissent by Justices Scalia and Thomas, confirming that the standard warning requirement applies as much in federal cases as in others. Professor Cassell, a well-known opponent of *Miranda*, submitted a special *amicus curiae* (friend of the court) brief in *Dickerson* at the invitation of the justices because the federal government's lawyers in the Justice Department—then under the Clinton administration—had refused to argue that § 3501 was constitutional. A Website on which Cassell argues that *Miranda* should be overruled is still available.[78]

———•————————•—————————•———

Summary

The exclusionary rule's mechanism of punishing cops by freeing criminals has never been popular, so courts have diminished its effect with many exceptions. At this time, some legal scholars and Supreme Court justices are openly working on an entirely new Fourth Amendment theory to use in judging the "reasonableness" of searches. The *Miranda* warning also has many critics because it keeps some confessions out of court and in other cases causes suspects to assert their rights to remain silent and consult with a lawyer. A statistical argument that *Miranda* did in fact slow down the rate at which police departments solve crimes has been made persuasively. Attempts to undo *Miranda* have been in progress since 1968 but, to date, none have been successful.

"Profiling" Makes Prejudice Official

P rofiling had a memorably painful effect on Master Sergeant Rossano Gerald of the U.S. Army, as he told a congressional hearing in 2001. He was driving with his 12-year-old son, Gregory, when Oklahoma state troopers pulled him over, questioned him insultingly, searched his car with a drug-sniffing dog, and caused $1,000 worth of damage by partly dismantling his car in search of secret drug compartments, before finally deciding he was not a criminal. Gregory was locked inside a car in intense summer heat and was frightened by the dog, with lasting emotional effects.[79] Former Congressman J.C. Watts told an interviewer he was once pulled over six times in one day while driving in his home state of Oklahoma.[80] Both Watts and Gerald are African American, and both happen to live in Oklahoma. The unfairness they experienced, however, happens to people all over the United States.

A lot of police work is done through pretextual stops and arrests—that is, the use of a minor offense as an excuse to stop or hold someone for further investigation. Traffic stops for speeding or other minor offenses are common pretexts: Traffic laws are so easily violated that, often, the question is not who breaks the law, but who gets stopped for doing so. If police making pretextual stops single out members of minority groups more often, how many innocent people are being unfairly humiliated, and how many majority-group criminals are going free?

The word *profiling* means different things to different people.

This chapter and the next discuss "profiling," which can be defined broadly as the practice of singling people out because they fit a certain description. *Profiling* is a relatively new term, but the question of when to single out certain people has always been central in search and seizure debates. *Terry* v. *Ohio*, for example, regulates profiling in the sense that it lets an officer confront a person based on suspicion rather than on solid evidence, but this is permitted only if the suspicion is based on "articulable" reasons—that is, only if the officer can put into words why suspicion was justified beyond the level of hunch.

> • **How closely should a profile fit someone to justify a *Terry* stop?**

In American conversations the word *profiling* can mean different things. Some speakers use the terms *profiling, racial profiling*, and *racism* interchangeably, for example, "Of course I was the one they stopped. The other drivers were white. I was profiled." *Profiling*, however, can also be used to describe the painstaking work of detectives, such as investigators hunting a serial killer. Such investigators would likely say they were working scientifically, that they could not afford to let prejudice skew the accuracy of their work. Favorable uses of the word *profiling* received a boost from the film *The Silence of the Lambs*, in which the heroine is described as an FBI profiler.[81]

Just because detectives use methods they consider to be scientific does not mean that they are right, however. Profilers guessed completely wrong about the perpetrator of the 2002 sniper murders in the Washington, D.C., area. During a three-week period of obsessive television news coverage, as random sniper attacks against Washington residents continued, some "expert" news commentators told the public to look for a young white loner. Instead, authorities finally arrested John Allen Muhammad, 41, and Lee Malvo, 17, a duo of African descent who had formed a close surrogate father-son relationship. As of this writing, Muhammad was appealing a death sentence and Malvo had been sentenced to life without parole but faced the possibility of the death penalty.[82]

Some right-wing commentators overtly argue that members of minority groups *do* more often commit crimes and therefore should be treated with more suspicion. They point to statistics that show that disproportionate numbers of arrests or reported crimes are alleged to have been committed by members of minority groups, especially African Americans. One answer to that statement is that when people of a certain category are suspected and searched more often and live their lives under closer official scrutiny, anything they do wrong is more likely to be discovered. The greater suspicion thus leads to a self-fulfilling prophecy. Another answer is that when people suffer discrimination all their lives, they have less to lose by breaking the law and less to gain by obeying it. Yet another answer is that people's attitudes about race may affect when and how they decide to report crimes.

What if, for whatever reason, the figures do reflect a genuinely higher rate of crimes committed by African Americans? Shouldn't individual people still be treated as individuals, not collectively punished as members of a category? A group of

Northeastern University researchers working for the Justice Department in 2000 put it this way:

> Just as we do not allow insurance companies to charge differential life insurance rates to women because they live longer than men, we ought not to allow empirical racial profiling to impose costs on the entire community of color. It would be unfair to stigmatize an entire community based on the conduct of a few. By allowing police to use race as a factor in determining whom to stop-and-search, many innocent Black and Hispanic individuals are subjected to searches.[83]

Profiling has an ugly history behind it.

Attempts to predict criminal behavior "scientifically" have an ugly history. In the nineteenth and early twentieth centuries, academics gave respectful attention to the pseudoscience of "physiognomy," the false idea that people's physical features could predict whether they would commit crimes. Writings like those of the Italian professor Cesare Lombroso made prejudice seem "scientific" by labeling facial features that were typical of unpopular ethnic groups as "criminal."[84] Beliefs about criminal tendencies being inheritable contributed to another pseudo-science, eugenics, which recommended variously more and less brutal ways of removing "bad" categories of people from the human population. It has been argued that such beliefs helped make the Nazi genocide possible.[85]

Biometrics, the science of cataloging human physical mea-surements, had its origins in the same late-nineteenth-century European criminology that produced Lombroso. A Paris detective named Alphonse Bertillon invented a biometric system based on measurements of body characteristics: the shape of the ear, forehead, nose, left foot and so on, plus blood type and color of hair and eyes. Some of Bertillon's ideas are used today in identification technology. Bertillon himself was disgraced by a

Racial profile policy not well defined

A new federal policy that bans racial profiling is being criticized by advocacy groups for minorities as not being tough enough to end the practice.

Guidelines DO . . .

☑ Allow border security officers to consider race in preventing threats to national security

☑ Prohibit law enforcement officers from using race in routine activities, such as traffic stops

Guidelines DON'T . . .

☒ Require agency to monitor their own compliance

☒ Require collection of data on who is being stopped and why

☒ Apply to state or local officials, only federal authorities

☒ Ban religious and national-origin profiling

SOURCE: Department of Justice

AP

In June 2003, the U.S. Justice Department issued guidelines intended to end the use of racial profiling by federal officials. The above Associated Press graphic summarizes some features of those directives.

mistake he made in the most notorious profiling case of the nineteenth century: He testified as a handwriting expert against Alfred Dreyfus, a French military officer accused of spying. A document apparently written by a spy had been found, and Dreyfus was one of several officers in a position to have written it. Of all the possible suspects, he was the only one accused, largely because he was Jewish. After many years of nationally wrenching controversy, another officer confessed to being the spy, clearing Dreyfus and proving that Bertillon and the many other accusers had been wrong.[86]

There are other profiling stories in American history. One concerns the Palmer Raids of 1919–1920, when a series of unsolved bomb attacks were blamed on immigrant political extremists. The raids, named after then-Attorney General A. Mitchell Palmer, were nationwide roundups of immigrants who had actual or suspected left-wing sympathies. At the height of this "red scare," federal authorities shipped 249 Russian citizens to Russia on the so-called "Soviet Ark," dumping them in the middle of that country's civil war in midwinter.[87] When the 1941 Japanese attack on Pearl Harbor brought the United States into World War II, federal officials afraid of spying and sabotage "evacuated" about 120,000 Japanese Americans from the West Coast, together with some Italian and German immigrants, under the infamous Executive Order 9066. Most of them spent the war in desert barracks behind barbed wire, essentially living as prisoners.[88]

During the Jim Crow era in the American South—from the collapse of Reconstruction in the 1890s through the civil rights movement of the 1950s and 1960s—what would now be called racial profiling was routine, often through selective enforcement of vaguely worded laws. Today, when claims that police are acting unfairly toward African Americans or other members of minority groups are made, the police are sometimes accused of following this old practice.[89]

Extreme profiling cases still do happen in the United States. One emerged recently from the small town of Tulia, Texas, where 46 people, most of them African American, were arrested on drug charges because of one undercover agent, Tom Coleman, who accused them without anything to back up his word. Later, questions about Coleman's honesty emerged. He was indicted on perjury charges, and the governor pardoned 35 people who had been convicted in these cases. One arrestee, Freddie Brookins, Jr., told a reporter after his pardon, "What hurt the most was that the people in the courtroom and on the jury knew me and knew I hadn't done it," he said. "All of it had to do with race. It's a stupid way to try to get people out of town."[90]

Profiling allows prejudice to interfere with properly impartial police work.

The racially motivated traffic stop is probably the classic example of unfair racial profiling in the United States. It is an old, bitter joke that some people are arrested for "driving while intoxicated" and others get arrested for "driving while black (or brown)." Many African-American families make "the talk" part of a son's upbringing—the conversation, as the boy reaches teenage years, about the need to respond calmly, politely, and with motionless hands in full view "when, not if" a police stop happens.[91]

In the 1990s, police racial profiling received new public attention after several notorious incidents, including the 1991 beating of Rodney King by four Los Angeles city policemen[92] and the 1999 police killing of African immigrant Amadou Diallo, who was shot when he pulled out his wallet and the officers mistook it for a gun.[93] In the Southwest, a profiling scandal surrounded "Operation Pipeline," a multistate campaign against drug couriers by the federal Drug Enforcement Administration (DEA). There, critics said, officers trained by the Pipeline project were blatantly singling out Latino drivers while claiming that the "drug courier profiles" they worked from were racially neutral.[94]

Civil rights and criminal defense lawyers had long found it difficult to prove that stops were racially motivated in individual cases. In one of the great civil rights breakthroughs of the 1990s, some lawyers started searching police departments' overall statistics of stops and arrests and finding discriminatory patterns. In a sense, this was a use of computerized profiling technology to monitor the police themselves.[95] David A. Harris argues that computerized crime-monitoring systems like New York City's Compstat should also look for patterns of incidents and complaints that may indicate problem officers.

They discovered that, in fact, some groups of officers, such as New Jersey highway police and U.S. Customs agents at airports, were choosing to stop members of minority groups more often than whites, in proportions that did not make good police sense, given the percentage of searches that resulted in discoveries of drug smuggling or other major illegality. In New Jersey, "searches in 2000 conducted with the subjects' consent yielded contraband, mostly drugs, on 25 percent of whites, 13 percent of blacks, and only 5 percent of Latinos."[96] A state study of New York City "stop and frisk" practices found that African Americans made up 25.6 percent of the New York City population but were subjects of 50.6 percent of police stops; "The NYPD 'stopped' 9.5 blacks for every one 'stop' which resulted in the arrest of a black, 8.8 Hispanics for every one 'stop' that resulted in the arrest of an Hispanic, and 7.9 whites for every one 'stop' that resulted in the arrest of one white."[97] Public interest in statistical evidence of racial profiling grew during the late 1990s, augmented by the filing of lawsuits. The evidence led to several congressional hearings in 2000 and 2001.[98]

• Can your skin color affect how much you are trusted?

Racial profiling at the national security level can also be worse than useless. On Christmas Day 2001, an Arab-American man in his 30s, with a book in his pocket called *The Crusades Through Arab Eyes*, boarded an American Airlines plane carrying a weapon. He presented a form on which he claimed to be a U.S. Secret Service agent. It happened to be true. His name was Walied Shater, and he was on his way to Dallas to continue his job guarding President Bush. The security staff did not believe him. *Newsweek* magazine reported that Shater's attorneys were accusing American Airlines of "illegal racial profiling" because they questioned his identity and told him to leave the plane.

The magazine added, "Lost in the shouting is the fact that some top federal sleuths view profiling as a way to let bad guys slip through. 'Profiling is just bad police work,' says one U.S. Customs Service official."[99] In other words, an obsessive security focus on certain categories, such as young Middle Eastern men, can help ill-intentioned people trick the authorities by playing against expectations. In fact, U.S. Customs Commissioner Raymond W. Kelly testified at a 1999 congressional hearing that drug smugglers do play against type, for example, by having drugs carried by children or hidden in wheelchairs.[100]

The hearing at which Kelly testified presented evidence that Customs officials were searching minority travelers out of proportion to their numbers, focusing especially on women of African descent. The hearing was held at the request of Congressman and civil rights leader John Lewis (D-GA). Lewis quoted research by a Harvard professor showing that "a Black woman traveler is 20 times more likely to be stopped and intensively searched than is a white woman." Two women testified at the hearing about health-damaging ordeals they had suffered while detained by Customs officials who wrongly thought that they had swallowed drugs.[101]

After this hearing, Commissioner Kelly decided on his own to ban searches based on race from the Customs Service. He changed training and supervision to guard against informally race-based decision making, put strict limits on medical exams, and set a two-hour limit on detentions without access to phone calls or other outside contact. The result was an 80 percent drop in the number of body searches and a 38 percent increase in drug seizures.[102]

Professor David A. Harris

…There is a relationship … between where you look for things and where you are likely to find them. If you look in the cars of African-Americans and Latinos, most often that is where you will find the stuff and that is who you will arrest.… If we thought that 40-year-old white law professors were likely to have more contraband and we could figure out a way to identify them from a distance, I guarantee you that within 3 years the statistics for 40-year-old white law professors would show many more arrested. It is that simple …

Source: *Racial Profiling* hearing, testimony of David Harris.

Senator Russell Feingold (D-WI) introduced an antiprofiling bill, S. 989, in summer 2001 and held hearings on the measure that August. The bill would have formally banned racial profiling, requiring programs to stop the practice at all federal law enforcement agencies and in state and local agencies that receive certain federal grants. The bill stalled after August 1. September 2001, of course, is when the terrorist attacks on New York and Washington, D.C., persuaded many legislators that police agencies should be granted more freedom, not less. A proposed "End Racial Profiling Act of 2004" was, however, pending in Congress as of this writing.[103]

List making does more harm than good.

A newer kind of profiling (for the United States) is the "watch list" or "gang database." For some years, urban police departments have gathered computerized lists of young people that they suspect of being involved in gangs. Groups concerned about police practices and minority groups' rights say that minority teenage boys and young men are often listed unfairly, sometimes on the basis of their clothing, neighbors, or associates, and without evidence that they have committed any crime. Contrary to the usual notion of "innocent until proven guilty," it can be difficult for people who appear on such lists to find out what official has the power to consider taking them off the list. In the 1990s, Latinos, Asians, and African Americans turned up disproportionately on a list of more than 20,000 "suspected gang members" in Orange County, California.[104]

List making is also a controversial practice at airports and customs checkpoints. A 70-year-old woman named Johnnie Thomas discovered in spring 2002 that her name was on a master terrorist list because a suspected murderer—a complete stranger to Mrs. Thomas—had used the alias "John Thomas Christopher." She made a long string of phone calls to government offices, and, when she took her next flight, the problem seemed to have been solved. On her way home from that same trip, she was put through special searches again. She told *The New Yorker*, "Something different happens every time."[105] In June 2003, there were news reports that men named David Nelson were getting "red flag" security treatment at airports because their very common name appeared on a list of potential terrorists.[106] The ACLU has complained of the federal government putting people on "no-fly" lists. Among other incidents, it cited a case in which peace activists arriving for a flight were first told that their names appeared on a no-fly list and then were allowed to travel, but were singled out for special searches.[107]

In the winter of 2002–2003, more than 1,000 Middle-Eastern immigrants were arrested, reportedly for immigration violations, when they appeared to register with the Immigration and Nationalization Service under a new federal requirement. Some faced deportation as a result.[108] The ACLU estimates that, in all, 3,000 to 5,000 people, "almost entirely Arab, South Asian, or Muslim," have been detained by the Justice Department since September 11, 2001, and "most have been deported or allowed to leave the country. None of the detainees has been charged with any terrorism-related crime."[109] However, courts are increasingly allowing investigation and hearing process to happen in secret—arguably in violation of Constitutional principles—so it is now difficult to know how many are held or what they are suspected of doing.

- **Is it unfair profiling to suggest that very religious people may behave in extreme ways? Does it matter if no particular religion is specified?**

Summary

To one person, "profiling" is the same as racism. To another, it is the careful work of detectives or security staff who must avoid prejudice for the sake of accuracy. Defining the word itself can be the beginning, not the end, of the argument. Some very scientific-sounding pronouncements have been made in defense of raw bigotry, and seemingly impartial police stops—for example, for violating the speed limit, or for customs questioning—can happen to members of minority groups more often than to others. List making as a form of profiling is of particular concern: People sometimes find that they have been put on airport security "watch lists" or in "gang associate" databases without ever being formally accused of wrongdoing, and because being placed on a list is not the same as a criminal charge, there may not be a formal procedure to get one's name cleared, either. The profiling debate became more intense after the September 2001 terrorist attacks, especially regarding the several thousand Muslim, Arab, and South Asian immigrants who have been detained with little or no explanation and in many cases forced to leave the country.

Profiling and Prejudice Are Different

It is a kind of profiling when police and prosecutors get to know the culture, language, and habits of a community in order to protect it against crime—and yet the result, far from being racist, can be culturally sensitive protection against culturally specific crimes. Consider the knowledge required to investigate and pursue "*notario*" fraud. In this common swindle, people who may or may not be licensed as notaries in the United States advertise themselves in Spanish under the term *notario* to exploit a quirk of language, law, and history.

The law of the United States, which derives primarily from England, makes a notary a person with relatively little training and authority. Spanish law, and the law of many countries that were colonized by Spain, however, recognizes a distinguished figure called a *notario público* who gives legal advice and also has judgelike authority to determine whether documents are legally valid. A Mexican notario público, for example, is a lawyer who has passed a rigorous additional training and selection process. Consequently, thousands of immigrants from Spanish-speaking countries have paid people who advertised themselves as notarios to represent them on American legal matters, especially immigration cases, that only U.S. lawyers are trained and licensed to handle. Some people have lost important cases because they trusted notarios who did not know or care enough to do the work right.

Consider, then, the role of a police officer investigating notario fraud: Some of the victims may have needed legal help because they were in trouble with the law. Some may have questionable immigration status or may come from authoritarian countries where it is prudent for even law-abiding people to avoid the police. It would help if the investigating officer spoke Spanish, understood the meaning of "notario público" in the victims' countries of origin, and made clear that the investigation had to do with the notario and not the victims' immigration papers.

Is it ethnic profiling for a police department to assume that notario fraud happens most among Spanish-speaking immigrants? Perhaps, but is it racism? It may be different, and better, than the kind of profiling that treats all Spanish-speaking immigrants with suspicion, but isn't it still a type of profiling?[110]

Profiling is merely learning from experience.

Profiling, in the sense of watching people's known behavior to guess at their unknown actions or intentions, is a universal practice. This is true not just for police and security officers, but for anyone passing a stranger on the street or interviewing an applicant for a job or in any other example of what earlier generations called "judging character."

Profiling does not necessarily have to do with discrimination against members of social or ethnic categories or even with law enforcement. It is a kind of profiling when poker players watch each other for "tells," gestures such as blinking or covering the mouth that may suggest that a player is bluffing. It is also, in a sense, profiling when an auditor or journalist searches a list of expenses for hints at corruption, or when a doctor checks for occupational illnesses based on a patient's work history.

- **Is it fair for stores to refuse to let in more than two teenagers at a time?**

Some profiling methods have unpleasant histories, but all sciences grow out of improvements over past mistakes. Biometrics came out of the nineteenth-century physiognomy tradition, which also gave pseudoscientific endorsements to prejudices of the time. Then again, modern chemistry has achieved trustworthy results although many of its founding discoveries came from medieval alchemists' unsuccessful attempts to turn lead into gold.

Measurements of people's physical features are now used to identify people as a supplement to photographs and fingerprints. Photographs and fingerprint images have appeared for many years on identity cards and in police "mug shot" books. Biometrics takes the same idea a step further by gathering additional data about people and recording it in computers. The computers can then be used to check for a match between new and old data, for example, to confirm that people entering a building are who they claim to be or to scan a crowd for wanted criminals. One machine lets people through a door if it recognizes unique patterns in the irises of their eyes, which is arguably no worse than having a unique key to one's own front door.[111]

Impartial profiling is possible.

Some arguments say that rational, honest profiling is really the opposite of prejudice. A prejudice is a belief held regardless of the truth, and the whole point of profiling is to find patterns in accurately perceived facts. One argument of this type is that profiling can be done by systematic scientific processes in which prejudice plays no part. Another is that police or investigators have to see people as they are, which means seeing people not only as individuals, but also as members of cultural, ethnic, or other categories.

In 1999 congressional testimony, U.S. Customs Commissioner Raymond W. Kelly said that customs agents considered many behavior factors in deciding whom to search in airports—for example, people who avoided eye contact or who bought airline tickets with cash on short notice.[112] There is still some risk of unfairness in picking people out this way: A person avoiding eye contact may simply be depressed and a cash ticket purchaser may have an innocent preference for not using credit cards. If these patterns also tend to be characteristic of drug smugglers, then in such cases officials arguably have reason to take a closer look.

- **Do people sometimes act guilty when they are not?**

This hearing was the one at which Customs took criticism for focusing on minorities generally and black women in particular. Kelly said, "I think you have to factor in where the travelers are coming from." For example, he said, flights from Jamaica are a likely source of drugs.[113]

The Customs Service responded by replacing worse profiling with better profiling. Customs involved supervisors and staff lawyers more closely in search decisions, kept better records, trained agents more carefully in both searches and cultural interaction, allowed subjects of searches to make calls within two hours of a stop, and bought new equipment that made less intrusive searches more easily. Kelly said that the new policies reduced the number of personal searches "from just over 43,000 searches in 1998 to just over 9,000 in the year 2000" but drug finds increased. "Those numbers showed us that we could identify narcotics traffickers without trampling on the rights of the law-abiding public."[114]

In the area of air security—an issue different from Customs concerns—U.S. transportation safety officials developed a passenger screening system called CAPPS II that made a point of disregarding race and ethnicity while screening travelers' other personal data for potentially dangerous profiles.[115] It was criticized in several very different ways: Liberal and conservative civil libertarians said that it could endanger privacy and other civil rights[116] and at the same time some right-wing commentators, openly supporting discrimination, found it foolish *not* to single out Arab or Muslim travelers for suspicion.[117]

> • Considering that, on average, members of minority groups tend to have lower incomes, would it be nondiscriminatory to stop older cars on highways more often than newer ones?

Fair profiling can be based on unscientific street experience.

"Based on my training and experience" is a common phrase in police officers' court testimony. An officer may use it, for example, to anticipate a defense attorney's suggestion that the officer

In the News

News report, mid-2001, on the profiling of a drug smuggler from Ecuador who had swallowed balloons containing a kilogram of heroin.

The case of a recent arrival to JFK [Airport] from Ecuador illustrates how the new system works. The man said he flew to New York to see the sights. But when pressed by a Customs inspector, he couldn't name a single sight, not even the Statue of Liberty. He claimed to be a professional photographer but knew nothing about lenses or light. He said his ticket was purchased in Chile, but records showed it came from Uruguay. And he had no idea what the ticket cost or whether it was paid for by credit or with cash.

Source: *S989* hearing, Statement of Raymond W. Kelly, p. 107, quoting Lori Montgomery, "New Police Policies Aim to Discourage Racial Profiling," *Washington Post,* June 28, 2001.

stopped a suspect based on mere hunch or stereotype and not "specific and articulable facts that, taken together with rational inferences from those facts, reasonably warrant that intrusion" as required by *Terry*.[118]

"Training and experience" can translate as a kind of profiling that simply uses knowledge of life and behavior to recognize a nervous tremor in a voice, a fishy detail in a story, suspicious last-minute travel, or the smell of marijuana. This kind of profiling may have nothing to do with discrimination based on immutable (unchangeable) characteristics like race. For example, a good officer, social worker, nurse, or doctor needs to be able to recognize the kinds of stories that victims of domestic abuse tell about injuries when they are trying to protect the people who hurt them.

- **How much deference should be given to an experienced police officer's gut feeling about a suspect?**

Heather Mac Donald, a member of the right-wing Manhattan Institute, presses a similar point farther, arguing that police stop people based on their professional experience and therefore are not acting on prejudice. Rather than defend profiling in so many words, she tends to phrase her arguments as defenses of police officers embattled on one side by crime and on the other by civil rights advocates. To her, accusations of racial profiling come from people who would rather not admit that the profiled people have characteristics police officers should rightly view as suspicious.[119]

Some defend racial profiling as good for the group although individually unfair.

A number of right-oriented magazine journalists, through publications such as the *National Review*, the *Weekly Standard*, and the *City Journal* of the Manhattan Institute, have argued openly that racial prejudices have truth in them, a view not necessarily shared by other advocates of profiling. The "stereotypes contain truth" position maintains that people entrusted with security work can only do their jobs properly if they apply more suspicion to categories of people who are stereotyped as more dangerous —for example, young African-American men in cities and Middle Easterners in airports. They argue that anyone who claims otherwise is out of touch with reality, afraid of giving offense, or too concerned with individual rights to respect the interests of the larger public.

In a congressional hearing on profiling, Johnny L. Hughes of the National Troopers Coalition offered an unusually blunt public defense of racial profiling as justified by statistics at a congressional hearing in March 2000. Other witnesses at that hearing presented statistics that showed that highway patrol officers had been stopping drivers on the basis of race. Hughes offered no explanation for the stops other than the drivers' race, but he argued that even stops based on race could be fair, because officers' experience showed that, on certain highways, the drug couriers tended to belong to certain ethnic groups.[120]

- **Is it possible to prove that any person's motives are free from prejudice?**

Similarly, the *Weekly Standard* published a column in mid-2001 titled "The Tragedy of Racial Profiling: It's Unjust— and It Works." The column began by acknowledging that stereotypes are sometimes wrong; the author displayed indignation, for example, that, after his own home was robbed by a black intruder, police officers suspected a respectable African-American neighbor just because of his skin color. Then, however, he pointed to statistics that appeared to show that "blacks" commit more than their share of crimes: "While only 13 percent of the population, blacks commit 46 percent of all robberies and 21 percent of rapes . . ."[121] He gave no source for these figures, but the federal Bureau of Justice Statistics report of its 1999 crime victimization survey, the most recent as of his writing, does show similar figures for "perceived race of offender" in survey responses that described "single-offender victimizations."[122] Some figures Tucker attributes to the New York attorney general's report elsewhere in the article are, however, incorrect,[123] and it is a commonplace that reports of crime are not always accurate.

> • **Is there a difference between claiming that members of a certain group should be suspected of crime more quickly, and claiming that members of the group are bad people?**

An interesting variation on the "stereotypes contain truth" claim is the view that it is a legitimate part of policing for officers to treat people differently based on characteristics that can at least be portrayed as voluntarily chosen, such as poverty, unorthodox lifestyle, or unpopular political opinion. Most forms of admitted racial or religious discrimination are pretty clearly illegal, at least if practiced by a government representative like a police officer, but it is harder to prove a violation of law where discrimination is based on a characteristic such as poverty.

Well-intentioned efforts against prejudice can get in the way of police work.

Some police officials argue that trying too hard to be fair can make police departments less effective. One version of the argument is that members of minority groups tend to be poorer than members of the majority and crime tends to be worse in poor neighborhoods; in order to protect the law-abiding victims of crime who also live in poor neighborhoods, the police have to spend more time there.[124] Then there is the argument that officers who are told to second-guess their own hunches may not stop even a suspect who is probably guilty for fear of being seen as prejudiced. Yet another argument is that a genuinely ill-intentioned (and dishonest) suspect has everything to gain from claiming to be a victim of prejudice.

In the 2001 hearing, a Fraternal Order of Police representative argued that antiprofiling requirements, in requiring officers to document more characteristics of people they encounter, may cause officers to think *more* about race, as well as wasting their time with paperwork.[125]

A more backhanded argument is that, whatever the police managers' personal opinions, they may have to deal with "malicious compliance" from rank-and-file officers—that is, sarcastically literal-minded obedience to orders that they consider foolish. Cincinnati police officers staged an informal work slowdown—a systematic group sulk—in which they avoided aggressive policing in mainly African-American neighborhoods, claiming that they could not confront criminals adequately there without being accused of racism. Crime increased in those areas.[126] Malicious compliance is a genuine risk in the United States, considering that local police departments to a great extent set their own policies, and individual officers in the field have tremendous discretionary power.

It is worth profiling and tracking potentially dangerous people to protect the rest of the public from harm.

When U.S. soldiers finally captured Saddam Hussein in 2003, the *Washington Post* reported that it was with the help of "link diagrams," "a strategy similar to that pioneered by New York City police in the 1990s, who cracked down on 'squeegee men' only to discover that they knew about far more serious criminals. . ." In the Hussein case, the U.S. investigators told the *Post* that they started by gathering generic information about a large number of people who trusted each other and eventually learned enough to focus on the closest associates of the man they wanted.[127] Investigation, detention, and interviewing methods might, of course, have been different under constitutional authority within the United States, but the common factor was the basic investigation tactic of figuring out how people were related to each other, even if at first the information did not seem immediately important.

By itself, figuring out relationships is not really profiling; it is just investigation. Where profiling comes in—profiling understood as singling out people based on memberships in categories—is in deciding whose associations are worth studying in the first place.

California gang databases have been criticized by civil liberties groups, but they have also helped protect the public from some genuinely dangerous criminals. Database software known as CAL/GANG has been credited with helping to solve a number of crimes by spotting connections among possible accomplices. A 1998 report in *Government Technology* magazine gave a glowing review to the system. A CAL/GANG match for the nickname "Bolo" provided the clue that made it possible to convict 14 young men of gang rape.[128]

As the use of computerized watch lists expands, some safeguards are moving into place. As of this writing, the federal Transportation Security Administration was working on "Secure Flight," a new air passenger screening system that would compare passenger data with no-fly and watch lists, but would also create a passenger advocate to respond to complaints by people who believed they had been wrongly or mistakenly put on the lists.[129]

Of course, it all comes down to the old familiar tensions between the individual and the group, between one person's right to be "left alone" and another person's hope for greater safety, and between the virtue of trust and the frequent necessity of suspicion.

Profiling is a commonsense necessity in antiterrorism and immigration law enforcement.

The questioning of the 5,000 immigrant men after September 11, 2001, is a classic example of profiling and a controversial one because some see it as an example of ethnic prejudice and others as a realistic investigative effort. Some local police departments refused to help the FBI with this project. The Portland, Oregon,

police said that the interviews would violate local privacy laws. The San Francisco police said that it would be bad for community relations. The police in Fremont, California, decided, although the ACLU asked them not to, to take part in the interviews in hopes of making them proceed more smoothly and respectfully in an effort to preserve good community relations between the police department and Fremont's "Little Kabul." Police Chief Craig Steckler told a reporter, "The FBI's going to do the questioning whether we're there or not, and I'm stuck with the problems—the ACLU's going to forget Fremont." [130]

> • **Is it fair to pay special official attention to arriving visitors from a country whose government is hostile to the United States?**

Columnist Steven Brill found that the interviews at least did not go as badly as civil libertarians had feared. He wrote in *Newsweek* that there had been earlier complaints about rude, threatening FBI men who barged into houses and asked personal questions such as "How often do you pray?" This time, the agents asked respectfully for help and advice and showed culturally appropriate courtesies such as offering to remove their shoes at interview subjects' homes. Some of the men among the 5,000 told Brill that the agents politely asked if they knew anyone who might be a terrorist or might know something about the attacks. This was an improvement on earlier experiences. Nevertheless, one interviewee said, "They were very polite, but you still feel violated by having someone from the FBI knock on your door. . . . You submit, because you figure they'll be watching you if you don't, but it was not pleasant." [131]

Summary
Just as not all people understand "profiling" to mean the same thing, not all defenders of profiling defend it in the same way.

Some say that profiling can be fair. Others say that it is necessarily unfair but still justifiable. Some supporters of profiling argue that it can be reasonable to treat some people differently because of their race. Other supporters of profiling find that serious investigative work is only possible by setting aside stereotypes of big human categories. An important distinction —one at the edge of the definition of profiling—is between the practice of singling people out because they fit a general description and the more specific practice of learning about a community in order to serve its law-abiding members well.

Existing Legal Protections Are Not Stopping Unfair Policing

The famous Rodney King police beating case is an example of an injustice that could not be addressed by the exclusionary rule. First King was not charged with a crime in connection with the beating and the exclusionary rule works by throwing improperly collected evidence out of criminal trials. Second, the mere dropping of criminal charges would not have compensated King for his serious injuries.

King's story began in March 1991, when California Highway Patrol officers saw him driving too fast and signaled him to pull over. King, who was intoxicated, kept driving but was eventually cornered by Los Angeles Police Department officers who had joined the chase. The LAPD men ordered King and his two passengers to get out of the car and lie prone. The passengers obeyed; King did not. The famous videotape, taken by a bystander, shows LAPD officers then beat and kicked King and gave him electric shocks with a police Taser, continuing after King had stopped all movements that could be seen as resisting. His injuries included broken bones in his face and leg.[132]

Unlike many victims of police brutality, King won money in a civil rights lawsuit. This was a considerable achievement: It meant he had advanced his case past the many possible pretrial objections and had persuaded a jury to take his word over the word of four police officers, which might have been difficult if a bystander had not taken the famous videotape. King suffered a serious injustice, but speaking comparatively (and more than a little cynically), his was a success story: At least the public recognized that he had been wronged, he got a court judgment in his favor, and he was not made to take the blame for the incident as well as the injuries. For plenty of others whose cases never make it onto television, even that much justice is more than they can expect.

Exclusion of evidence does not help people who never get to court.

Arguments that support the exclusionary rule tend to say that it helps keep the police honest. As discussed previously, it excludes wrongly obtained evidence from criminal trials, so a police officer theoretically knows better than to randomly search someone's house, for example, because the resulting evidence would be thrown out under *Mapp* v. *Ohio*; an officer knows that hurting suspects to make them confess would get the evidence thrown out under the Fifth Amendment *Miranda* rule.

Similarly, the "great writ" of habeas corpus, respected in old English law and imported into the U.S. Constitution, entitles people to bring challenges from inside jails or prisons to allege that they have been locked up unfairly. Theoretically, at least, sensible police or security agencies would never hold people without trial, because the courts would let them go free.

Chief Justice Warren knew all along, however, that the possibility of exclusion of evidence from criminal trials could not regulate American policing by itself. In 1968, in the Supreme

Court's *Terry* v. *Ohio* majority opinion, he wrote that the exclusionary rule should be used only to restrain police conduct up to a point, beyond which the practice of throwing out unconstitutionally obtained evidence would make policing more difficult without stopping abusive officers. He added that his *Terry* opinion, although confirming police officers' power to make investigative stops, "should in no way discourage" courts from using additional approaches to block police abuses. He also saw the available ways to get around the rule. He wrote:

> The exclusionary rule has its limitations, however, as a tool of judicial control. . . . Regardless of how effective the rule may be where obtaining convictions is an important objective of the police it is powerless to deter invasions of constitutionally guaranteed rights where the police either have no interest in prosecuting or are willing to forgo successful prosecution in the interest of serving some other goal.[133]

Fast forward to 1997. Oliverio Martinez is riding a bicycle near a vacant lot in Oxnard, California. Two officers stop him for questioning. They frisk him and find a knife. Martinez fights with them. An officer shoots Martinez several times. Martinez is taken to an emergency room, injured badly enough that he expects to die. Ben Chavez, a patrol supervisor, questions Martinez in the emergency room while he is in pain and fearing death and without reading him any rights, although Martinez repeatedly asks him to stop. Under questioning, Martinez admits to drug use and to taking an officer's gun during the fight. He survives his wounds but remains blind and is paralyzed from the waist down. He files a civil rights lawsuit that alleges that Chavez violated his Fifth Amendment right against self-incrimination and his Fourteenth Amendment due process right against "coercive questioning." In 2003, the Supreme Court throws out his case, saying that none of Martinez's rights to fair questioning were violated because he was never charged

Translation of the Chavez-Martinez questioning (originally in Spanish), quoted in Justice Stevens's concurrence and dissent

O[liverio]. M[artinez].: I don't want to say anything anymore.

Chavez: No?

O. M.: I want them to treat me, it hurts a lot, please.

Chavez: You don't want to tell [sic] what happened with you over there?

O. M.: I don't want to die, I don't want to die.

Chavez: Well if you are going to die tell me what happened, and right now you think you are going to die?

O. M.: No.

Chavez: No, do you think you are going to die?

O. M.: Aren't you going to treat me or what?

Chavez: Look, think you are going to die, [sic] that's all I want to know, if you think you are going to die? Right now, do you think you are going to die?

O. M.: My belly hurts, please treat me.

Chavez: Sir?

O. M.: If you treat me I tell you everything, if not, no.

Chavez: Sir, I want to know if you think you are going to die right now?

O. M.: I think so.

Chavez: You think [sic] so? Ok. Look, the doctors are going to help you with all they can do, OK? That they can do.

O. M.: Get moving, I am dying, can't you see me? Come on.

Chavez: Ah, huh, right now they are giving you medication…

Source: *Chavez v. Martinez*, 538 U.S. 760 (2003) 786.

with a crime in court and adding that Chavez did not mistreat Martinez because he did not stop the emergency room staff from treating him.[134]

If Martinez had been charged with a crime, he could have objected that the confession was forced out of him and could have moved to suppress the evidence (have it thrown out of court) under the Fifth Amendment equivalent of the exclusionary rule that is spelled out in *Miranda*. Because he was never charged with a crime, however, the evidence that Chavez so painfully extracted was never used against him in court, so the right to exclude evidence was of no use.

Chavez v. *Martinez* illustrates rather dramatically that police have less reason to avoid mistreating a suspect who they do not expect will be formally charged with a crime. This is even more the case in small-scale, comparatively undramatic incidents in which police commit unreasonable searches and seizures without making arrests.

David Harris reports that, when police departments are preparing their statistics, they generally do not pay attention to the number of people they stop and search without finding anything illegal, because those stops do not cause the officers themselves any trouble, no matter the fear, loss, or inconvenience they might have inflicted on those searched. He quotes Professor William Stuntz of Harvard Law School as noting that "the police tend not to take account of costs they do not bear." [135]

Police searches and seizures that do not go to court can cause measurable losses as well as indignities. "Property sweeps" against the homeless are one kind of policing that inflicts losses without resulting in criminal charges. In a property sweep, police and cleanup crews impound or destroy property found at a campsite. Police have used the tactic more carefully in recent years because of activist pressures, but at least in the past cleanup workers would throw away things like sleeping bags and personal papers as "abandoned property" or "garbage," sometimes even when the owners were present.[136]

The exclusionary rule does not prevent official actions that can "punish" people without a trial or alongside a trial, such as towing a vehicle and refusing to return it until daily storage fees have risen into the thousands, issuing building-inspection citations for every arguable defect in a building viewed as a problem, or beginning civil forfeiture actions that take away property allegedly used in drug activity. (For civil forfeiture seizures, vehicle towing, and other situations in which the government takes private property, there is a Fourteenth Amendment due process right to a hearing, but not to all the rights of a courtroom trial.[137]) At the level of the official security agencies, what use is an exclusionary rule against a security officer who refuses to let someone board an airplane based on unfair profiling?

The exclusionary rule also could not stop police officers from sulking, as the Cincinnati officers did by staging a slowdown in neighborhoods where they had been accused of racism. Because the exclusionary rule works on the assumption that police officers want to put criminals behind bars, what can it do about officers who refuse to make arrests?

Civil rights remedies outside of criminal trials are too weak.

In the Rodney King case, a Los Angeles jury decided that the city should pay $3.8 million to King and $1.6 million more in attorneys' fees. The jurors also decided that the policemen who beat him should not personally have to pay anything. (By then, some were no longer police officers and two were in federal prison.) Officers who mistreat suspects often do not have to pay anything. It only speaks to the special importance of the King case that the officers suffered any loss at all. As it was, King went through a painful series of disputes with his lawyers and apparently ended up with about $1.9 million.[138]

There are a number of ways to bring civil rights lawsuits. King used the oldest, grandest, and often most powerful method: the federal claim under 42 U.S. Code Section 1983 for deprivation of civil rights "under color of" law. Section 1983 has an old and honorable but frequently sad history. Its basic text derives from the Civil Rights Act (or Ku Klux Act) of 1871. Congress passed it soon after the Civil War ended, in an attempt to protect the rights of newly freed slaves from corrupt local officials, but § 1983 came into vigorous, frequent use as part of the twentieth-century civil rights reforms. The 1961 Supreme Court case of *Monroe* v. *Pape* found that municipal governments, including local police, cannot be sued under § 1983. The Court changed its position in *Monell* v. *Department of Social Services* in 1978, saying that local governments can be sued where "execution of a government's policy or custom" causes the rights violation. Section 1983 is currently accepted as a way to sue local authorities, and local police are frequently named in such lawsuits. The Supreme Court created an equivalent means of suing federal officials with *Bivens* v. *Six Unknown Named Agents of the Federal Bureau of Narcotics* in 1971.[139]

Because racism is frequently alleged in § 1983 actions, the phrase "under color of" is sometimes misunderstood. Acting "under color of law" means using a claim of government authority to do something that may or may not actually be legal. Specifically in § 1983 lawsuits, though, it is not enough that the wrongdoer claims government authority: A hoaxer who showed a fake police badge could not be sued this way. Only acts attributable to "state action" justify § 1983 lawsuits, which means that the person accused of violating rights must be a government representative or employee.[140] Section 1983 applied in the Rodney King case, for example, because the people who beat King were uniformed, on-duty city police officers who acted as though it was their job to hurt him as badly as they did.

In a § 1983 police misconduct lawsuit, plaintiffs have to get past a series of high hurdles, including specific limits on prisoners' lawsuits,[141] strict jurisdictional limits, and various government and individual claims of immunity. A person or entity granted immunity in a § 1983 case does not have to face trial, let alone pay anything or submit to court orders. Section 1983 plaintiffs' lawyers routinely start by naming a lot of public entities and individual people as defendants, knowing that immunity findings will drop many of them from the case. It is possible to go to trial only if there are defendants left in the case after the courts' immunity decisions. (These immunities are among the barriers to suspects' rights that Akhil Amar has suggested reducing.)

Government entities are protected from § 1983 in various ways. The federal government cannot be sued under § 1983, although it can be sued in certain situations under *Bivens*. State governments cannot be sued in federal court because of the Eleventh Amendment and cannot be sued under § 1983 in state court because of a court-made doctrine that states are not "persons" as defined by the law.[142] Municipal governments can be sued under § 1983, although they cannot be made to pay "punitive damages," extra payments imposed as punishment for wrongdoing, beyond the actual value of the loss suffered.[143]

Lawmakers, judges, and prosecutors, among others, benefit from "absolute immunity" for any violations of civil rights that they may be accused of having committed as part of their official functions. Police officers normally do not get this protection for daily actions on the job, but when they are testifying in a criminal trial they have absolute immunity—even if they lie in court.[144]

Most litigated is the trickier principle of "qualified immunity," which applies to individuals such as police officers or school officials rather than to governments.[145] Described very generally, qualified immunity shields public employees such as police from being made to pay compensation to injured parties out of their own pockets if they can show that they were following their understanding of law or policy—unless they could have been expected to know better. The rough phrase "could have been expected to know better" is substituted here for concepts that have been defined in great detail through 30 years of high-stakes hairsplitting. Qualified immunity is still loosely called "good faith" immunity, based on the old idea that it protects officials who act "in good faith" without meaning to do wrong. Beginning in the 1970s, however, the requirements for qualified immunity shifted in a series of Supreme Court determinations.

The 2001 police misconduct case *Saucier* v. *Katz*, an important current standard, said that the court reviewing a §1983 case must first decide if the plaintiff's accusations add up to a constitutional rights violation. If so, the case said, the accused officer can still have qualified immunity if the allegedly violated right was not "clearly established." It said, "The relevant, dispositive inquiry in determining whether a right is clearly established is whether it would be clear to a reasonable officer that his conduct was unlawful in the situation he confronted."[146] Even if a constitutional right was definitely violated, officers get the benefit of the doubt if it seems possible that their violation of the law *could* have been an innocent misunderstanding, regardless of what they actually knew or thought.

In *Saucier*, the plaintiff, a political protester, was detained roughly by security officers but soon released without injury. The Supreme Court may have found it easy to rule against a protester with a relatively minor grievance, but the effect of precedent was such that it now makes lawsuits more difficult for more seriously injured parties. For example, *Saucier* was cited in the pro-police *Chavez* v. *Martinez* decision, a case in which the plaintiff suffered much more.

Guards in privately run prisons do not benefit from qualified immunity, so they are easier to sue under § 1983 than ordinary police or correctional officers are.[147]

Federal law makes it a crime for police officers to deprive people of rights under color of law.[148] Practically speaking, criminal charges are brought under this law only in extreme cases because prosecutors are reluctant to bring such charges and citizens called to serve as jurors in such trials tend to believe that they can trust the police. As much of the world learned in April 1992, a jury in Simi Valley, California, could not agree to convict the four officers who beat Rodney King of a rights violation even though they had the video in front of them. Anger at the acquittals caused major riots in Los Angeles.[149]

Two of the officers, Stacey Koon and Laurence Powell, were later convicted of criminal civil rights violations in a separate federal trial. They were imprisoned for 30 months, although the federal guidelines called for longer sentences, and these relatively short sentences were not changed by appeals that went all the way to the Supreme Court. Furthermore, by the time Koon and Powell completed their sentences, a *Los Angeles Times* editorial commented:

> Now, they are not broke. This is particularly true of Koon, because of national fund-raising efforts to pay his legal expenses and the debts of his family. By some estimates a defense fund set up for him and a trust fund set up for his family have raised at least $8.8 million, which is more than the $3.8 million King was awarded in his lawsuit against the city. How much Koon will actually pocket has not been made public—but it's quite likely more than he would have made had he obeyed the law and kept his job.[150]

Although the Rodney King case created a sense of injustice that filled a major city with flames and broken glass, it is overall an example of the civil rights legal redress mechanisms working largely as they were designed to work. King did prove to a court, and certainly to much of the public, that he was beaten unfairly; he did get money in compensation; prosecutors were willing to bring the officers to trial twice; two of the officers served federal prison time; and the Los Angeles Police Department was shamed into some policy changes that may have helped prevent other beatings.

A knottier problem for the civil rights community is what to do about less dramatic cases that do not engage public attention, where police misconduct has probably happened, but no charges are brought and the case is not clear-cut enough for a major lawsuit.

Privately funded organizations and volunteers can only help so much. Legal aid offices funded by the federal Legal Services Corporation have limited budgets and work under rules that restrict the types of cases that they may bring.[151] For-profit civil rights law firms exist, but the lawyers in them have to choose cases that will pay. Most victims of police brutality cannot afford to pay hundreds of dollars per hour up front, so these lawyers mainly work on contingency, which means a promised portion —often 30 percent—of any money won. Some civil rights statutes, including § 1983, also allow attorneys' fees to be claimed separately from the money that goes to the plaintiff. A private lawyer cannot afford to invest months of work in a case unless it seems likely to produce a fair-sized verdict or fee award, however. Lawyers have a good chance of making money from cases like Rodney King's, but not necessarily true for more ordinary "driving while black" cases. Even when there are serious, clear-cut police brutality injuries, a victim who also faces criminal charges will have trouble bringing a civil rights lawsuit unless the charges are first dropped or defeated in court. This can be difficult to achieve, especially because it often happens that people who have committed crimes are also mistreated by authorities. When both parties have done something wrong, juries may not be sympathetic. Not everyone has the sophistication to distinguish between the treatment a lawbreaker may seem to have deserved and the laws a police department is required to obey.

Class action cases, controlled in federal law by Federal Rule of Civil Procedure 23, are one way to address the problem of harm that affects many people in a way that makes it unlikely that any given person will sue. A § 1983 class action can allege a "pattern and practice" of rights violations against many people who are "similarly situated." Class action cases are financially and technically difficult projects, and those who set out to get landmark decisions risk getting an adverse decision that will hurt future similar cases.

Other remedies for police misconduct in state and federal law include applications for court orders that can have some of the effect, though not the complexity, of class actions; lawsuits under the more ordinary laws that govern compensation for injury or property damage; and administrative complaints of various kinds. In some towns, the only administrative complaint possible is one to the management of the police department. In others, it is possible to complain to other entities, such as independent police review boards. Larger cities may have community organizations or civil rights law offices that monitor police conduct.

Coordinated small claims court filings have had some success against homeless camp property sweeps. Small claims courts generally handle low-stakes cases in which people represent themselves. Each of the campers who had property taken or destroyed files a claim for a few hundred dollars—the value of the lost items plus modest compensation for resulting hardships such as sleeping outdoors with no blankets. They ask to have all of their cases heard at the same time. They may lose, but at least they can subpoena the officers who took their property to come to court and explain themselves.

It has been difficult to get the kind of big court injunction that could change the way in which whole police departments work. One of the most memorable tries, *Rizzo* v. *Goode*, was defeated by the Supreme Court in 1976. In their local federal court, Philadelphia plaintiffs and civil rights lawyers got an injunction ordering detailed changes such as new language in police manuals. On appeal, the Supreme Court rejected it, saying that the purpose of an injunction is to prevent present or future harm and the people who claimed to have suffered mistreatment in the past did not show that city police behavior was continuing to harm them or likely enough to harm them in the future.[152]

In 2002, after a lawsuit alleging systematic long-term racial profiling and a Justice Department investigation, a court agreement setting out restrictions on Cincinnati police conduct was reached successfully. Its implementation, however, was affected by an unofficial police work slowdown.[153]

The courts are again letting the police make their own rules.

Policing has a number of purposes. Only one of them is investigation of reports of major crimes such as assault and robbery. Sociologists and criminologists have identified other purposes that include maintaining order, protecting people with high status, and enforcing conventional morality against activities such as drug use and prostitution.[154]

Scholar James Williams says that scholarship:

> suggests that the vast majority of police time is spent intervening in minor conflicts and disputes, managing indigent and "problem" populations such as the young, the unemployed, and the homeless, as well as engaging in a number of administrative and general social assistance duties. . . . The impetus for police involvement in the majority of these instances is not evidence, or suspicion, of a violation of criminal law. Rather, police attention is seen to be demanded by the perception that particular acts, or types of individuals somehow constitute a threat to the social order.[155]

Ordinary stops, searches, and seizures are the areas in which individual police officers have the most discretion—the most power to decide whom to stop. The more the courts trust police discretion, the more individual officers get to decide, if not what the law is, at least what "the rules" are to maintain order among particular people or in particular neighborhoods. That may be fine as long as individual officers behave reasonably, but from a civil rights perspective, it also makes abuses possible, and the United States is a country where laws are supposed to be made by elected legislators, not by unelected police.

One of the most influential articles ever written about policing contains a perfect example of a policeman enforcing rules that are not in any law book and in a comparatively benevolent way. "Broken Windows: The Police and Neighborhood Safety," was written in 1982 by two academic researchers on police practices, James Q. Wilson and George Kelling.

Wilson and Kelling told, with sympathy, how an "Officer Kelly" defined and performed his job as a foot patroller carrying out a "Safe and Clean Neighborhoods Program" in a rundown but busy neighborhood of central Newark. Kelly tolerated a certain level of disorder, but he made his own unwritten rules. For example, "Drunks and addicts could sit on the stoops, but could not lie down. People could drink on side streets, but not at the main intersection. Bottles had to be in paper bags." The researchers wrote, "Sometimes what Kelly did could be described as 'enforcing the law,' but just as often it involved taking informal or extralegal steps to help protect what the neighborhood had decided was the appropriate level of public order. Some of the things he did probably would not withstand a legal challenge."

This article has been widely quoted over the past 20 years by urban scholars, police, and politicians who feel that cities are made safer—or, at least, made to *feel* safer—when the police protect "respectable" people from "being bothered by disorderly people. Not violent people, nor, necessarily, criminals, but disreputable or obstreperous or unpredictable people: panhandlers, drunks, addicts, rowdy teenagers, prostitutes, loiterers, the mentally disturbed." [156]

The title came from Wilson and Kelling's application of research about tolerance for vandalism to a more general idea of policing. They wrote:

> Social psychologists and police officers tend to agree that if
> a window in a building is broken and is left unrepaired, all
> the rest of the windows will soon be broken. This is as true

in nice neighborhoods as in rundown ones. Window-breaking does not necessarily occur on a large scale because some areas are inhabited by determined window-breakers whereas others are populated by window-lovers; rather, one unrepaired broken window is a signal that no one cares, and so breaking more windows costs nothing. (It has always been fun.)

As Wilson and Kelling describe it, Kelly's behavior was a fairly reasonable use of police discretion, though he was using his law enforcement authority to enforce rules not found in any book. They do not tell if there was any difference in the way people of various races were treated, and they imply that Kelly did in fact treat poorer people more harshly than more prosperous ones, which may or may not be viewed as fair.

Now, consider the behavior of Officer Bart Turek in the 2001 case of *Atwater* v. *City of Lago Vista*. There, the Supreme Court found that Officer Turek of Lago Vista, Texas, did not break the law when he treated a woman more harshly than usual but in a way that was technically correct. Turek had stopped Gail Atwater's truck once before, thinking that her son was not wearing a seatbelt, but she had shown that he was in fact belted in. Later, Turek stopped Atwater for a minor seatbelt offense that would ordinarily have gotten only a ticket, but he insisted on taking her to jail and would have taken the children, too, if a neighbor had not stepped forward to care for them. She was booked and detained an hour before paying $310 in bail to get out. Afterward, Atwater admitted she had broken the seat belt law but sued, claiming that the officer's behavior was still so unreasonable it violated her Fourth Amendment rights. A five-member Supreme Court majority held the officer acted within the law.[157]

Justice David Souter's majority opinion in *Atwater* partly turned on the fairly narrow question of whether arrest was at all proper for a misdemeanor whose only prescribed penalty was a fine. The decision discussed larger policy implications in detail, however, and among other things claimed, "The country is not confronting anything like an epidemic of unnecessary minor-offense arrests." From a certain perspective, though, there may indeed be such an "epidemic," considering the way in which poor, minority, and otherwise unpopular persons are routinely arrested for comparatively minor offenses under policies such as the famously heavy-handed "zero-tolerance" policing in New York City.

Another recent case increasing police discretion is *Whren* v. *U.S.* in 1996, which found it that was not a Fourth Amendment violation when police officers used a minor traffic violation as a pretext to stop someone who they generically suspected of being up to no good. In the *Whren* case, officers in a "high drug area" noticed a man who drove away suspiciously fast after a long stop at a stop sign. The officers caught up with him, supposedly to warn him about traffic violations and in fact to check for drugs. The man did have drugs and was arrested. In a unanimously backed opinion by Justice Antonin Scalia, the Supreme Court refused to suppress the evidence on Fourth Amendment grounds and upheld the conviction.[158]

The problem, from a civil rights perspective, is that *Atwater* and *Whren* give more discretionary power to both the Officer Kellys and the Officer Tureks. It allows officers, whether acting in good faith or in spite, to use laws that govern minor offenses as a pretext or an excuse to punish people they consider troublemakers or to stop and search "usual suspects." *Atwater* and *Whren* help officers find excuses to treat people unfairly within the letter of the law.

Court decisions like these are backhandedly returning some of the power police once had to arrest people for "crimes of status," as punishment for any kind of behavior the police considered troublesome. Laws that punished certain vaguely defined statuses or behaviors, such as "being a disorderly person," "wandering or strolling around from place to place without any lawful purpose or object," or "blocking free passage" of a sidewalk were invalidated by a group of civil rights cases, the chief of which were *Shuttlesworth* v. *City of Birmingham* in 1965, *Papachristou* v. *City of Jacksonville* in 1972, and *Kolender* v. *Lawson* in 1983.[159]

These decisions established that it was not a crime to have a certain status. Officers who want to make an arrest must catch a person doing something specific enough that people can avoid doing it if they want to stay within the law. For example, laws that declare it a crime to be an alcoholic have been found unconstitutional, but laws that make drinking liquor in public a crime are still valid.[160]

"Broken Windows" and "zero-tolerance" policies depend on police having power to stop people for a lot of the same reasons that used to be covered by crimes of status, especially when it comes to crimes committed by poor and addicted people. Now, to be arrested for the crime that used to be called "being without visible means of support," a person has to be more creatively charged with drinking in public, "trespassing" in a doorway, or violating park codes that require keeping off the grass.

Gary Stewart, author of a *Yale Law Journal* article titled, "Black Codes and Broken Windows," argues that the police practice of enforcing unwritten rules about "order" and also the old "crimes of status" laws used to do this have origins in the racist laws and practices used to subordinate African Americans both before and after the Civil War.[161] Not coincidentally, two cases cited previously involved racially inflected uses of overly broad laws: *Shuttlesworth* cleared a civil rights activist who had been sentenced to six months' hard labor for "blocking free passage" of the sidewalk outside a department store. *Papachristou* cleared four people whose "crime" was apparently that they were African Americans and whites riding together in a car.

Stewart argues that, even since civil rights victories like *Papachristou*, there has been a consistent and continuing pattern in the United States of creating new vaguely written laws that can, in practice, be used unequally against members of minority groups. He sees the latest effort in this long tradition as being the civil injunction against "gang activity." This is a court order that can ban "gang members," who may or may not be accurately labeled as such, from spending time with "gang" friends, standing around outdoors, or any number of other ordinary activities. This can result in arrests for acts that normally are not considered crimes, a result with debatable historical resonance.[162]

"Zero-tolerance" policing labels people as criminals too easily.

"Zero-tolerance" policing is especially associated with the sudden severity of New York City police methods under Mayor Rudolph Giuliani, which was credited with making Manhattan safer and more attractive in the 1990s. As applied to public spaces—the New York subway, for example—zero tolerance is really a super-tough kind of "Broken Windows" policing. Officer Kelly kept a paternalistic eye on people without enforcing every law, but an officer enforcing a zero-tolerance policy with the goal of making a shopping street more respectable would at least set out to arrest or cite every person found in violation of public drinking or open-container laws.

William Bratton, the New York City police commissioner most associated with zero tolerance (he is now the Los Angeles police chief), started his New York career as head of the city transit police. He began by requiring strict enforcement of laws on minor offenses such as fare evasion. He reported, "We found that one out of every seven people that we arrested for fare evasion was wanted on a warrant, and one out of every 21 was carrying some type of weapon."[163]

That sounds good, but zero tolerance can mean that police stop everyone they suspect of carrying a weapon or acting suspiciously or "evasively"[164] and everyone they allege fits the general description of a suspect. If police are especially suspicious of people who belong to minority groups, it follows that more members of minority groups will be affected by zero-tolerance policies, as was found in the New York state attorney general's study of New York "stop and frisk" practices.[165]

Zero tolerance can easily give a child a lifelong label. Some school districts have taken severe approaches to discipline that criminalize (label as crime) behavior that, in other places or other times, would have drawn a less record-damaging punishment such as detention.[166] Claims that school officials may be quicker to call the police for bad behavior when it involves minority students are sometimes made. In October 2002, a fight between black and Asian students broke out at a San Francisco high school. Students and their parents protested afterward that the police responded with unnecessary force and numbers and arrested not only the boys who fought but also a teacher who tried to videotape what happened.[167]

David Harris, in his book on profiling, criticizes the New York City zero-tolerance approach because of its lopsided effect on members of minority groups and prefers an approach to "community policing" in San Diego that he found more humane. According to his figures:

> Under San Diego's community and problem-oriented policing approach, crime also dropped in the 1990s—as it did in many other cities—but it dropped *more* than in New York. This occurred across all categories of crime, including violent crimes such as homicide. And whereas New York will be dealing with the legacy of the Giuliani administration's zero-tolerance policies for many years to come—including a sharp antagonism between the police and racial minorities, who feel that they bore the brunt of the mayor's enforcement policies—San Diego's police department has been traveling in the other direction.[168]

Another researcher, Judith Greene, made a New York–San Diego comparison showing that, from 1993 through 1996, crime decreased about the same in San Diego as in New York, but

San Diego reduced the number of arrests whereas New York increased them. She further reported that complaints filed with New York's civilian review board for police conduct "increased more than 60 percent between 1992 and 1996." She adds, "William Bratton has attributed this increase in complaints of police misconduct to the increased number of police officers on the streets. His critics point out that the increase in complaints far exceeded the increase in personnel during this period."[169]

The public is too willing to grant new official powers.

After the September 2001 terrorist attacks, grants and claims of police power increased. Legislators and the public largely approved these in hopes of making daily life more secure.[170] From a civil liberties perspective, especially one concerned with search and seizure law, these changes risked allowing the people entrusted with the public's safety to behave lawlessly.

Emergency measures directed at specific evils changed the whole criminal justice system several times in the twentieth century. Such special measures included Prohibition, the various anti-"Red" campaigns, the FBI's notorious "COINTELPRO" campaign against radical groups and its spying on Dr. Martin Luther King, Jr., in the 1960s, and the War on Drugs in the 1980s and 1990s. The War on Terrorism, it can be argued, fits this pattern.[171]

- **Now that the 2001 attacks have happened, do the barriers to domestic surveillance created in the 1970s seem like a luxury the United States cannot afford?**

Even before September 2001, the proverbial pendulum was swinging to the right, increasing the search, seizure, and surveillance powers of federal officials. These powers had been restricted in a number of important ways during and after 1976, in response to public outrage at disclosures of the government's past political spying. By 2000, there was a controversy over how to adapt existing wiretap laws to the problem of monitoring

Tapping in and turning up the heat

Among other effects, the Patriot Act of 2001 broadened law enforcement's ability to investigate crimes using electronic means:

- Payment information of e-mail and Internet customers, such as credit card or bank account numbers, can be obtained with a subpoena.
- E-mail and Internet service providers are permitted to disclose customer records to law enforcement in cases of an emergency involving immediate risk of death or serious physical injury.
- Non-content information, such as e-mail addresses and Internet addresses, can be identified with a subpoena in the same way phone numbers of incoming and outgoing calls are identified.

Wiretap applications

Government requests for wiretap authority are rarely denied by judges.

Year	Authorized	Denied
1990	922	0
1991	941	0
1992	966	0
1993	1,182	0
1994	1,200	0
1995	1,139	0
1996	1,197	1
1997	1,276	0
1998	1,443	2
1999	1,521	0
2000	1,190	0
2001	1,491	0

SOURCES: U.S. Department of Justice; Center for Democracy & Technology   **AP**

The 2001 USA PATRIOT Act increased the number of legal wiretaps or searches available to law enforcement officials. The popularity of electronic forms of communication necessitated the expansion of search laws to govern law enforcement's abilities to surveil e-mail and Internet activities.

e-mail on the Internet, and civil libertarians were arguing that the FBI was interpreting technical problems to allow itself too much access without proper warrants.[172]

Major changes after 2001 involved one of the 1970s safe-guards: the Foreign Intelligence Surveillance Act of 1978 (FISA).

FISA required a "wall" between ordinary U.S. law enforcement work on one hand and, on the other, national security intelligence work on spying and terrorism when it required investigations inside the United States. Courts could grant warrants more easily for FISA wiretaps and searches than in ordinary law enforcement cases. The word *foreign* in the law's name reflected the assumption that security-type investigations would have to do with the behavior of foreign governments.

The USA PATRIOT Act weakened this wall in several ways, one of which was to increase the kinds of wiretaps or searches that could get a judge's permission under the easier FISA standards rather than the strict ordinary ones.[173] A groundbreaking federal court battle in late 2002 and early 2003 established that the Justice Department could use the easier FISA process to spy on people in the United States as a way of gathering evidence for criminal prosecutions, and not only in cases that involve foreign intelligence.[174] In 2003, the FBI issued guidelines that allow its agents to work more closely with the intelligence services and make it likely that they will conduct more secret wiretaps and searches under FISA.[175] Meanwhile, the Justice Department gave up some of its 1976 restrictions on FBI spying methods. One controversy concerns the Justice Department's November 2001 decision to lift its self-imposed ban on undercover attendance at political and religious meetings.[176]

The USA PATRIOT Act is possibly even more notorious for helping investigators get court orders more easily to demand information from third parties, such as libraries, marketing companies, and Internet service providers, that are not normally involved in security or law enforcement.[177]

There are related further concerns over the Homeland Security Act of 2002, which not only combined many government functions in a new superagency, but also made it easier for investigators to gather and "mine" data from public and private sources. Among other provisions, this law made it extremely difficult for people to learn details or sue if their privacy rights were violated by businesses such as Internet service providers that disclosed customers' information to the government.[178]

Soon after the September 11, 2001, attacks, the federal Justice Department began to claim that it could keep terrorism suspects behind bars without trial or normal rights such as access to lawyers. It claimed that it could hold people who might know something about terrorism as "material witnesses" to make them testify before grand juries and that it could label U.S. citizens suspected of terrorist involvement "enemy combatants" and thereby strip them of all legal rights—even the right to see a lawyer.

> • **Have you said anything today that could make a suspicious person think you wanted to break a law or rule?**

The cases of U.S. citizens Jose Padilla and Yaser Esam Hamdi, both U.S. citizens held as enemy combatants, were decided in June 2004 along with *Rasul* v. *Bush,* a habeas corpus challenge to the Guantánamo Bay "enemy combatant" detentions. To the great relief of civil libertarians, the *Hamdi* v. *Rumsfeld, Rumsfeld* v. *Padilla,* and *Rasul* v. *Bush* decisions did not allow the government to lock up people on its mere say-so. The decisions said that people held under the enemy combatant label do not have rights to full criminal trials, but the *Hamdi* opinion said that they do have the right to consult lawyers, see evidence against them, and have hearings "before a neutral decisionmaker." Liberal constitutional scholar Ronald Dworkin warned, however, that the Court was making it possible for the government to meet formal requirements by holding hearings that were unfair to the prisoners in practice.[179]

Reports about the alleged cruel treatment of prisoners in Guantánamo and other special national-security detention places have surfaced.[180] Some of the reports allege that prisoners have been tortured to extract information. Next to these stories, it may appear strange that the Court has just formally preserved *Miranda*'s comparatively fussy rule about reminding prisoners of their right against self-incrimination. At present, it appears that the United States operates a two-level system of imprisonment, in which constitutional rights such as habeas corpus and the Fourth Amendment apply mainly to ordinary criminal suspects, but such rights are not available to people being held without trial under special status. There is likely to be debate in the coming years over which distinctions between the two levels continue to exist and how many people are placed on each level.

As of this writing, there were various proposals before Congress that call for greater police powers, less restriction on eavesdropping, and more extraordinary powers to put people suspected of terrorist activity—citizens as well as immigrants—into special categories with fewer rights rather than treating them as ordinary criminal suspects.[181] These also will be subjects of considerable continuing debate in future years.

Summary

The exclusionary rule may protect people accused of crimes from being convicted in court, but criminal trials do not redress all police misconduct. Civil rights lawsuits and administrative complaints offer some hope to victims of police misconduct, but courts have become increasingly permissive in finding that police officers who act unreasonably or pretextually are merely doing their jobs. Some urban policing protections have focused on clearing public spaces or restraining problem groups of people, which erodes respect for the idea that people are responsible for their actions and should be treated as equal individuals, not as members of a group or category. Meanwhile, a parallel set of national security–related search and seizure laws is developing more or less outside conventional constitutional protections.

Restricting Search and Seizure Power Too Much Hurts Public Safety

Vigorous use of police search and seizure powers, alongside friendlier types of "community policing," drove drug dealers out of the Boyd Booth neighborhood in Baltimore. A showpiece Comprehensive Communities Program involving a federal grant, the city police, and local community organizations, helped Boyd Booth neighbors take back local public space from drug dealers who had made them afraid to complain. According to a report by Jeffrey Roth and George Kelling, the program succeeded not just by enforcing drug laws, but by indirect efforts that included police foot patrols, physical efforts to make spaces uncomfortable for dealing or hiding drugs (for example, by boarding up vacant buildings), letting the dealers know that they were watched, supporting continued recovery efforts by ex-addicts, and keeping the neighbors engaged in a campaign to use the streets for more law-abiding purposes.

The program operated on several levels, not all of them involving police investigations or arrests. For example, it organized cheerful community picnics on notorious drug corners—an activity that neighbors could join without fear of provoking revenge attacks from the dealers, but one that did force the dealers to do their business elsewhere. Private legal organizations brought "nuisance" lawsuits on behalf of neighbors against the owners of drug-troubled properties. (An article that Kelling cowrote argues that nuisance lawsuits brought by prosecutors "signal our society's rejection of the exaggerated value placed upon individual rights and liberties—at the expense of community interests, civic duties and the need for order in a democratic society." [182])

Extra police patrols, including "order maintenance" methods and the full use of police information-gathering tactics, were an important part of the cleanup, as were city housing code enforcement efforts in court. Patrol officers specially assigned to the area made a point of making local friends, which helped them get local business owners' permission to watch trouble spots from inside buildings, for example. As these officers talked with local people, they learned a lot about how the neighborhood worked; saw a lot; got a lot of tips about crime, from children as well as adults; and were able to tell fellow officers where and how to make a lot of arrests. One officer told the story of a drug dealer who "gave him another dealer's stash out of outrage that someone would store drugs in front of his mother's house." The same officer performed possibly controversial "order maintenance" functions—for example, "He breaks up groups of loitering teenagers he finds in the street." [183]

Successes like the Boyd Booth cleanup support the argument that police powers can be used vigorously and successfully in a poor neighborhood on behalf of the local community, not in spite of it. Naturally, people who fear arrest are never likely to welcome the police wholeheartedly, but when the orderly members of a neighborhood feel that the police are representing and respecting them, it is difficult to argue that increased restrictions of police powers would serve the greater good.

The rule of law suffers when police are over-restrained.

Police officers operate under a heavy load of contradictory laws and expectations imposed by law and public opinion. Criminologist Jerome Skolnick writes:

> Democracy's ideological conflict between the norms governing the work of maintaining order and the principle of accountability to the rule of law provides the justification for various demands on the police. A member of the force may be expected to be a rule enforcer, parent, friend, social servant, moralist, streetfighter, sharpshooter, and officer of the law.[184]

Meanwhile, they have to pursue criminals who break all the rules, and although they are bound to respect the freedoms of suspects, they also have to protect the freedoms of people who would otherwise be at the mercy of gangsters, abusers, and other bullies. From the officers' point of view, an unequal battle results. *Battle* can literally be the right term in some areas: Officers in the United States have to be prepared for dangers that may include automatic weapons fire.[185]

Ordinary patrol officers must keep up on the latest criminal court decisions and can still get in trouble for misunderstanding them despite protections such as those in *Saucier* v. *Katz*. When they create a record of an investigation or arrest or testify in court, they have to know certain aspects of the law very well to avoid objections by defense attorneys. The heaviest court-authored shocks to police departments came from 1960s procedural due process decisions like *Mapp* and *Miranda*, but the process goes on: One day an appellate court or the Supreme Court issues a decision and suddenly the patrol routine has to change.

Police officers have to base quick decisions on incomplete information. Cases like that of Amadou Diallo, where a man's quick movement in producing his wallet startled officers into shooting him to death, involve split-second decision making. In the Diallo case, officers were looking for a man fitting Diallo's general description who was believed to have raped 51 women. A New York City officer not involved in the Diallo case itself wrote, "I wondered if Amadou Diallo died because the N.Y.P.D. thought too little of the South Bronx, or too much. Whenever I heard about the 41 shots, I thought about the 51 women raped."[186]

There are too many anti-police lawsuits.

When police departments face a lot of complaints that allege prejudice or brutality, does that skew officers' judgment? When it comes time for a snap decision that could save a life, take a life, or both, will a patrol officer make the wrong choice out of fear of provoking a lawsuit? Previous chapters have explored the idea that allegations of police racism may cause officers to stop confronting crime aggressively in neighborhoods where the accusations are made. One term favored by conservatives for this kind of passivity is "depolicing." Another is *retreat,* a word used, for example, by Senator Orrin Hatch (R-UT), talking about the police slowdown and resulting crime increase in Cincinnati.[187]

Chief William Bratton, formerly of New York City and now of Los Angeles, is famous for arguing that a police force can only make real progress in reducing disorder if its members are willing to risk provoking complaints.

Heather Mac Donald has become known for angry answers to the civil rights rhetoric of groups such as the American Civil Liberties Union (ACLU), whom she describes as "professional cop-haters."[188] Her 2003 book, *Are Cops Racist? How the War Against the Police Harms Black Americans,* argues that civil rights complaints reduce policing in neighborhoods that are mainly African American, and that law-abiding residents of the same neighborhoods are especially likely to be victims of crime if the police do not intervene to protect them. (The book limits itself to allegations of racism in majority-black neighborhoods and the issue of antiblack racism; it does not address claims of discrimination based on other minority statuses.) In arguing that civil rights complaints are unfair to police, Mac Donald cites figures that state that African-American officers stop people in the same ethnic proportions as white officers, and she quotes some black officers as taking offense at the claim that their policing or that of their colleagues is racially prejudiced.

"Spitting on the sidewalk" stops and arrests can help the public.

It is not known who first said that Robert F. Kennedy would prosecute a mobster even for "spitting on the sidewalk," but it is a fact that, when he served as U.S. attorney general, he used the

William Bratton, now the Los Angeles chief of police, in his book about changing New York City policing in the 1990s

It is important to define "police brutality." We defined brutality as unnecessary behavior that caused broken bones, stitches, and internal injuries. But those were not the figures that had gone up significantly. What had risen were reports of police in appropriately pushing, shoving, sometimes only touching citizens. We were taking back the streets, and it wasn't easy work. . . . A lot of the "brutality" was reported by those people engaged in illegal behavior and looking for a bargaining chit. In three years there had been over 15,000 complaints of all types: brutality, disrespect, etc. During that same period the department had made almost a million arrests.

William Bratton with Peter Knobler, *Turnaround: How America's Top Cop Reversed the Crime Epidemic*. New York: Random House, 1998, p. 291.

Migratory Bird Act to jail one reputed mobster, got another convicted of lying on a federal mortgage application, and had many more prosecuted for tax fraud. For this, he had a precedent in the downfall of legendary Prohibition-era Chicago gangster Al Capone. In 1929, President Herbert Hoover set up a special interagency "Get-Capone Squad" that eventually got Capone behind bars for tax evasion.

In the 1950s, Bobby Kennedy began to pursue gangsters as part of his work for Senate investigating committees. As U.S. attorney general during the presidency of his brother, John F. Kennedy, he continued to look for ways to convict reputed gangsters and mob-tainted labor leaders, most memorably Jimmy Hoffa of the Teamsters Union. Kennedy showed almost obsessive dedication to bringing down these figures. He asked the Internal Revenue Service (IRS) to do "saturation type" examinations of their tax returns. He got different federal agencies— for example, the Federal Narcotics Bureau and the FBI—to share information on key crime bosses. He sent both the FBI and the IRS to plant microphones in offices. "In the end, 60 percent of all organized crime cases in these years were tax cases."

Some lawyers and civil libertarians of the time objected to Kennedy's approach without necessarily pitying his targets at all. In their view, "he was deciding that people were guilty and then looking for something they could be found guilty of. He was convicting them not for their real crimes but for slips that anyone might have made. Beginning with the criminal rather than with the crime led to selective justice." Kennedy's supporters argued that conventional methods could not produce clear proof that high-level racketeers were responsible for their underlings' crude violence and that the mobsters always had plenty of money to pay for good defense lawyers. The only way to make any progress against such men was to use any available legal hold over them.[189]

More recently, "spitting on the sidewalk" arguments have been made to support pretextual approaches to vaguely suspected people in the War on Drugs and the War on Terrorism; for example, closing down crackhouses through strict enforcement of building codes, or arresting Muslim immigrants for minor immigration paperwork problems in order to look for connections to fundamentalist radicals. Similar arguments have been used for Chief Bratton's style of zero-tolerance street policing. In October 2001, Attorney General John Ashcroft invoked Robert Kennedy's spirit in the newly urgent context of fighting terrorism. He told a meeting of city mayors, "Robert Kennedy's Justice Department, it is said, would arrest mobsters for 'spitting on the sidewalk' if it would help in the battle against organized crime. It has been and will be the policy of this Department of Justice to use the same aggressive arrest and detention tactics in the war on terror." [190]

To take a recent example of antiterrorism prosecution, in 2004, an Eritrean-born U.S. citizen, Abdurahman M. Alamoudi, pled guilty to felonies of unauthorized travel to Libya, immigration fraud, and "a tax offense involving a long-term scheme to conceal from the IRS his financial transactions with Libya and his foreign back accounts and to omit material information from the tax returns filed by his charities." These offenses might not sound so dreadful in themselves, except that the plea agreement contained a "statement of facts" that said that Alamoudi had been secretly moving large amounts of money as part of a plot to assassinate the Saudi crown prince. Other charges against Alamoudi were dismissed under the agreement, which also provided for him to cooperate with investigators. IRS Commissioner Mark Everson was quoted in the announcement as saying, "We will vigorously pursue all violations of the law, including lying to the IRS, in going after terrorism." [191]

It is hard to imagine police work without pretextual stops and arrests—that is, the use of a minor offense as a pretext to single someone out who is the focus of police attention for other reasons. Police may stop a car for speeding because they guess that the driver may be carrying drugs, and they may issue a jaywalking ticket to a visibly homeless man to let him know he is not wanted in a prosperous shopping district. Before the due process revolution of the 1960s, their right to do this was simply not questioned in the courts. More recently, in the aftermath of landmark due process cases, police take their authority for pretextual stops and arrests from court decisions like *Whren* v. *U.S.* and *Atwater* v. *City of Lago Vista.*

The practice of looking for serious crimes by policing minor offenses does have a greater effect on people who, because they have less money, spend more of their time in public places or in heavily policed neighborhoods. This can lead to charges of hypocrisy—but should a cop look the other way out of pity on seeing a homeless person in a doorway with a crack pipe? Is it unreasonable to patrol more strictly in popular downtown shopping streets where public drunkenness could alarm visitors to the city?

Sometimes a genuinely important arrest is made because a stop for a minor offense gives an officer a reason to take a closer look. The arrest of Oklahoma City terrorist Timothy McVeigh is one example. On the morning when the Alfred P. Murrah Federal Building was destroyed, a state trooper stopped a car for speeding. He then saw that it had no license plate and that the driver appeared to be carrying a gun; he seized the gun and then discovered that his suspect also had an illegal knife. It was only after he made the arrest on these relatively minor driving and weapons charges, and, in fact, just hours before a court hearing that might have gotten McVeigh released on bail, that officers discovered that their arrestee matched drawings of the terrorist suspect.[192]

Every time a civil liberties complaint questions the authority of police to stop people for small reasons, it raises the question of what other crimes the failure to make such stops would keep from being discovered or prevented. Many people who are neither civil rights activists as in *Shuttlesworth* nor challenging racist ideas as in *Papachristou* come under police suspicion because they are doing something genuinely unpleasant or illegal in public. Someone who is begging may simply be needy, but he or she may also be using begging as a cover for steering drug addicts to a dealer. Someone who is as yet doing nothing wrong, just walking down a street of closed businesses late at night, may be getting ready for a break-in. Some situations like this may not be suspicious enough to justify a *Terry* stop. To the (endlessly debated) extent that an experienced police officer manages to spot a crime in the making and scare the would-be criminal into a confession, the public safety may in fact be served, whether the Constitution is obeyed or not.

Chief Bratton introduced a literal "spitting on the sidewalk" approach in New York City: the zero-tolerance practice of arresting people for any breach of public civility that could be viewed as breaking a law. Bratton criticizes the older-style focus on responding to calls and solving reported crimes as "reactive policing."[193] His own view partakes of the "Broken Windows" idea that even small signs of disorder, in themselves harming nobody, can lead to a general climate of disrespect for law that makes serious crime more likely. Bratton argues that his order-maintenance policing led to a drop in crime in New York City that was not explained by any of the theories his opponents devised. He states that birth rate patterns were not producing smaller numbers of young men as some said, the criminals were not all in jail, the gangs had not suddenly reached a truce, the replacement of crack by heroin as drug of choice had not especially mellowed the addict population . . . and yet New York City crime figures were down.[194]

New threats and technologies call for new search and seizure laws.

Commentators in favor of greater police authority have frequently paraphrased Justice Jackson's comment that the Constitution, while it protects rights, is not "a suicide pact."[195] When people's lives have to be protected from real dangers, sometimes it is important for the government to exercise more power than might otherwise seem reasonable.

A classic way to think about such questions is to consider thought-provoking extremes, scenarios that one hopes will happen rarely, if at all, but may clarify one's moral standards. If police have captured a terrorist who knows where an attack is about to happen, what should they be allowed to do to get that person to talk, if getting information quickly would prevent hundreds of deaths? Are hundreds of lives really worth less than respect for the Eighth Amendment prohibition of cruel and unusual punishment?[196]

In an epidemic, should a government be able to order people with the disease to stay in their homes? In Singapore in 2003, officials enforcing a quarantine for the Severe Acute Respiratory Syndrome (SARS) virus placed Web cameras in front of ill people's homes and telephoned them at random intervals, ordering them to step in front of the camera to prove that they were still at home and not out potentially spreading the disease.[197]

What about saboteurs from a hostile military force caught on U.S. soil? That situation came up in 1942, when the United States was at war against Nazi Germany. Seven members of the German military, all of whom had lived in the United States and one of whom claimed to be a U.S. citizen, were caught by the FBI after they landed on beaches in New Jersey and Florida with orders to sabotage military industries. They were tried before a military commission, not an ordinary court, and the Supreme Court found it proper to deny them access to ordinary civilian courts.[198]

When the Fourth Circuit Court of Appeals upheld the treatment of Yaser Esam Hamdi (the Supreme Court has since ruled otherwise), Attorney General Ashcroft commented in response:

> Today's ruling is an important victory for the president's ability
> to protect the American people in times of war. Preserving the

president's authority is crucial to protect our nation from the unprincipled, unconventional, and savage enemy we face. Detention of enemy combatants prevents them from rejoining the enemy and continuing to fight against America and its allies, and has long been upheld by our nation's courts, regardless of the citizenship of the enemy combatant." [199]

A lot of the recent arguments for more police authority have to do with the ability to make and share lists of facts or names that may not mean much by themselves but that could be terribly important when assembled to show a bigger picture.

A year after the September 11 attacks, congressional investigations had begun to bring out evidence that U.S. intelligence agencies had observed several signs of impending terrorist attacks but had failed to draw the correct conclusions. These revelations suggest that better management and more communication between intelligence agencies might both have helped prevent the attacks.[200]

Among the most criticized provisions of the PATRIOT Act are those that call for seizing information from third parties such as libraries. These are not entirely new. In 1978, the Supreme Court established that police investigating a crime can obtain a search warrant to forcibly seize evidence from a third party who is not suspected of wrongdoing. In *Zurcher* v. *Stanford Daily*, police used a search warrant to enter the offices of Stanford University's student newspaper and look for news photos of a violent protest in which demonstrators had injured policemen. The newspaper challenged this action on Fourth Amendment and freedom of the press grounds, arguing that local prosecutors could have simply ordered them to bring the evidence to court. Nevertheless, the Supreme Court held that the police and prosecutors acted legally in using the search warrant.[201]

Sooner or later, the question becomes what to do when moral and constitutional principles conflict with the immediate need to protect the public from people with bad intentions. Constitutional legality and security are not always opposites, but sometimes they have tense relations. In a world where catastrophically harmful terrorism is now a serious reality, there are extremely persuasive arguments to be made that rights can be less important than physical protection of the public.

Summary

Police have to do a hard job that requires tough snap decisions, and they cannot be second-guessed all the time or their work suffers. Lawsuits that allege police brutality can damage officers' morale and prevent them from pursuing crime aggressively. "Broken Windows" and zero-tolerance strategies, which emphasize order-maintenance policing, help law-abiding people feel safer and sometimes create important pretexts to catch serious criminals. The controversial law and policy changes made since September 2001 are justified in the light of new threats and technologies.

Lonely Detectives, Thin Blue Lines, or What?

J oan Didion's book *The White Album* begins, "We tell ourselves
stories in order to live." She goes on to say that we turn
events into stories with morals in an attempt to make sense of
a world that does not make sense.[202] Small wonder, then, if we
also see real events in terms of the stories we know or have
heard. When one person's reality is radically different from
another's, we fall back on stories to decide which version rings
true. Telling stories is only part of an argument about something
as complicated and important as the Constitution's restraints
on policing. Stories supplement and humanize cold lists of
big-picture facts, but they should not be treated as a substitute
for considering the big picture.

Arguments about policing, as on any divisive subject, can
turn into storytelling contests. In thinking of a police-suspect
confrontation on a lonely Los Angeles street, it is possible to

think of the *Onion Field* kidnap and murder, in which two cynical cop killers put the state through six years of court proceedings based on claimed violations of their Fourth Amendment rights. It is also possible to think of the Rodney King beating, in which the worst crime was committed by the officers, not the suspect, but the officers were acquitted by a jury and only two of the four served prison time. Both stories engage the emotions. Both stories, unfortunately, are true. One story could be used to argue that police officers risk their lives heroically for an ungrateful society that values suspects' rights over justice. The other story could be used to argue that police officers can and do abuse suspects without fear of consequences. Neither of these arguments would tell the whole story. An argument that consists of people telling stories to each other is no substitute for a reasoned discussion of how best to apply constitutional principles in order to be as fair as possible in all kinds of cases, involving all kinds of personalities and moral pressures.

Americans' personal experiences with crime and policing vary fundamentally from one person to the next. People who have seen bad police behavior can wonder if they live in the same country as those who believe in Officer Friendly. A victim of crime who sees a robber's case get thrown out of court may complain that the system is kind to criminals. An inner-city tenant who calls the police but is treated like a suspect may wonder if officers see themselves as serving the whole public equally. Small-town homeowners may see the local police department as a useful, uncontroversial public utility and wonder what the fuss is about.

In 2003, a group of Oakland night-shift cops who had called themselves "the Riders" were tried on charges of abusing African-American suspects, planting evidence, and writing false police reports. Their accuser was a former rookie who testified that he had gone along with the lies and abuse for a while, but at some point had had enough and quit the department. Who was telling the truth? All summer the jury argued furiously—

the judge had to tell them to stop shouting insults—and they could not agree.

Two African-American alternate jurors watched the debates but were not allowed to take part. Afterward, they said that the jury was mostly suburbanites who had no experience of the way police behave towards minority Americans in tough neighborhoods like the Riders' beat in West Oakland. The jurors' identities have been protected in public, so assumptions about them may be unfair, but the alternate jurors' comments suggest that perhaps the people who voted to acquit the Riders were hearing a story about the nature of America that they did not believe could be true because it did not match their experience. Interesting, then, that the jurors turned to Dirty Harry, a fictional character, for help. The *San Francisco Chronicle* reported:

> At one point, using Clint Eastwood's "Dirty Harry" character, jurors debated the ethics of a cop who violates the law to save a person's life. Jurors also noted that Dirty Harry was a good cop pushed over the line by aggressive politically motivated bosses.
>
> "Some people have trouble believing these cops can do anything wrong," said juror No. 6, who voted guilty on about 15 charges. "I personally felt that these cops were not all bad but they clearly went too far in some situations. Many fellow jurors had trouble accepting that." [203]

The "Dirty Harry" persona emerged from anger at the 1960s Supreme Court issued suspects' rights decisions including *Mapp* and *Miranda* and cases like the *Onion Field* kidnap and murder. Resentment of rule-bound bureaucracy within police departments became a popular theme. The film *Dirty Harry* introduced a brave, honest policeman who shows undisguised contempt for the new requirements to protect suspects' rights. Elements of Dirty Harry's character reappear in many television cop dramas. There is often a dedicated, streetwise officer embittered by having to step carefully within the law while pursuing clever, dangerous lawbreakers or who refuses to do his job by the book because he finds it necessary to fight an ugly world of crime with its own tactics. In real life, for the past 20 years or so, courts have increasingly granted exceptions to Fourth Amendment rules, so that officers' conduct is less restricted than it once was. Nevertheless, the idea of a brave crime fighter held back by petty bureaucrats endures.

American crime fiction has good reason to return to the conflict between the crime-fighting individual and the law-enforcing institution. The trouble, always, is that it takes a brave, clever pursuer, using flexible, unpredictable, rule-breaking methods to catch a genuinely dangerous criminal—but the last thing a democracy needs or wants is flexible, unpredictable, rule-breaking public institutions. Dirty Harry may look good on the screen torturing a villain, but a whole police force of Dirty Harries would be intolerable. If people think about crime fighting as something done by a lone hero against all the odds, they may want to give that hero as much power and courtroom leeway as possible. Still, anyone would think carefully before giving such license to a whole police agency, with its much greater powers and its unavoidable quotient of bad apples and nervous rookies.

In fact, a lot of popular fiction about crime and policing has to do with tension between institutional and individual ways of how to serve justice. It is true of real stories that catch people's imaginations and also of fictional detective and cop dramas. The theme appears throughout the classic detective-story tradition, starting with Edgar Allan Poe in the 1840s, to Arthur Conan Doyle's Sherlock Holmes stories at the turn of the twentieth century, to later twentieth-century masters like Dashiell Hammett and Raymond Chandler, to present-day writers like Walter Mosley. A lot of these stories feature the "Lonely Detective," who is often, though not always, a man working outside the system whose cleverness, bravery, and unorthodox methods are in competition against plodding official inquiries that are always inadequate—sometimes corrupt, sometimes rule-bound, always lacking imagination. Some of the stories, like Hammett's *Continental Op* series, make the hero a representative of a heroic organization. Hammett modeled some of these stories on his own real service with the Pinkerton detective agency. A Conan Doyle story, *The Valley of Fear,* was similarly based on a Pinkerton operation, and the plot involved one organization outmaneuvering another.[204]

Critics have suggested that people enjoy detective stories because they have the reassuring effect of solving the crime and distinguishing the innocent from the guilty.[205] Such clear differences between good and bad and guilty and innocent rarely emerge in real life, so it is a dangerous temptation to expect that police can guess correctly in advance who is guilty of a crime or that every story that involves crime and punishment will have clear-cut heroes and villains. Expecting fiction's clarity from messy reality can encourage the mentality of *Dirty Harry*: that some heroes are so firmly on the good side that even committing torture does not make them morally wrong and that some villains are so dreadful they deserve whatever they get. The rule of law does not work like that.

The police are relatively popular at present, in part because officers themselves became politicized in reaction against the 1960s rulings on suspects' rights. Their efforts have helped create support for the idea of law and order and sympathy for the problems that officers encounter. Professor Skolnick writes, "Crime and the police have, since the 1960s, become a public preoccupation. Like the cowboy, the cop has emerged as a mythic figure in the panoply of American folk heroes."[206] Police do serve the public bravely and well, but the less fashionable rights of the accused also need to be considered. Telling stories about the harm caused by crime is not a valid way to argue that the rights of the accused should be reduced. They are, after all, the rights of the *accused,* and accusations can be wrong.

On his University of Utah Website, Professor (now Judge) Paul Cassell, coauthor of the statistical study that criticized Miranda rights, shows proof of the extent to which police and "victims' rights" lobbying has become institutionalized in opposition to groups that advocate for the rights of the accused. Cassell was invited to submit his special brief supporting the legislative overruling of *Miranda* in federal prosecutions because the Clinton administration's Justice Department refused to take that position.[207] On his resource page with documents from the case, Cassell lists a large number of law enforcement and anticrime organizations among the groups that filed or endorsed amicus curiae briefs that criticized *Miranda*. These are just some of the names: the Fraternal Order of Police, the FBI Agents Association, the National Association of Police Organizations, the International Brotherhood of Police Officers, the Federal Law Enforcement Officers' Association, Americans for Effective Law Enforcement, Parents of Murdered Children, Arizona Voices for Victims, Citizens for Law and Order, and the Criminal Justice Legal Foundation.[208]

The Fraternal Order of Police brief begins by confidently claiming a better right to comment on *Miranda* than the legal experts who submitted other briefs:

> With all respect to those among Petitioner's amici who have some experience in law enforcement. . . those amici have far less experience than the rank-and-file membership of the F.O.P. in implementing *Miranda* in real-life situations that arise in front-line police work. Accordingly, the views of Petitioner's amici as to how *Miranda* operates in practice are of limited value.[209]

The FOP claim of superior moral authority is worth reading critically. The police union does indeed have members who have formed strong opinions on *Miranda* through long practical experience of street confrontations, and their stories are likely worth hearing—but a brief is persuasive, or not, on the strength of the legal argument it makes, not on the moral authority claimed by its backers.

Victims of civil rights violations, and victims of crimes, do often claim a superior right to speak because of their exceptionally painful personal experiences. Readers and debaters should keep in mind, however, that all these claims to have a better right to speak are ways of advocating legal rules that would apply to everyone by telling stories about particular cases.

Police stops, searches, and seizures are a rich subject for true-crime drama, so in conversations it may be easy to get drawn into exciting individual stories with apparent or actual heroes and villains, in which the moral of the story may seem to indicate clearly that the law ought to be different in some radical way. At such times, it is important to remember that one Constitution has to apply to all situations. A constitutional right that it seems quaint or risky to respect in one case may turn out to be a valuable protection against injustice in another.

Summary

Storytelling is an attractive way to make arguments, but sympathy for one person's problems is a dangerous way to arrive at a position on an issue like constitutional rights. When it comes to policing in particular, there are compelling stories that suggest that rights are respected too much and other equally compelling stories that suggest that rights are respected too little. Fictional police or detective stories, with their unrealistic moral simplicity, sometimes influence real life, as in an Oakland police misconduct case where jurors' conversations about the police-backlash drama *Dirty Harry* may have influenced a real acquittal of allegedly corrupt officers.

In a time when the profession of policing is popular and both police and victims' rights groups are politically active, it is important to also consider the rights of the accused and to consider carefully how constitutional rights need to serve as a protection for the whole public.

Introduction

1 Bureau of Justice Statistics Press
Release: State Prison Population Drops
in Second Half of 2001; Federal Inmate
Growth Continues. *http://www.ojp
.usdoj.gov/bjs/pub/press/p01pr.htm.*

2 See *California* v. *Acevedo*, 500 U.S. 565,
581-2 (1991) and articles cited therein;
Akhil Reed Amar, "Fourth Amendment
First Principles," 107 HARV. L. REV. 757
(1994); Carol S. Steiker, "Second
Thoughts about First Principles," 107
HARV. L. REV. 820 (1994); Tracey Maclin,
"The Central Meaning of the Fourth
Amendment," 35 WM. & MARY L. REV.,
197 (1993); Thomas Y. Davies, "Recover-
ing the Original Fourth Amendment,"
98 MICH. L. REV. 547 (1999).

3 J.C. Holt, *Magna Carta*, Cambridge
University Press, Cambridge, U.K.,
1965.

4 *Miranda* v. *Arizona*, 384 U.S. 436
(1966), citing *The Trial of John Lilburn
and John Wharton*, 3 HOW. ST. TR. 1315
(1637).

5 Leonard W. Levy, *Origins of the Bill of
Rights.* New Haven, CT: Yale University
Press, Nota Bene, 2001, pp. 151–159;
Maclin, "Central Meaning," pp. 218–219;
L. Kinvin Wroth and Hiller B. Zobel,
eds., *The Legal Papers of John Adams*,
vol. 2. Cambridge, MA: Harvard
University Press, Belknap Press, 1965;
Colin Rhys Lovell, *English Constitutional
and Legal History.* New York: Oxford
University Press, 1962; *Wilkes* v. *Wood*,
98 ENG. REP. 489 (C.P. 1763); *Entick* v.
Carrington, 19 HOW.' ST. TR. 1065,
1813 ed.

6 *Barron* v. *Baltimore*, 32 U.S. 243 (1833);
Kermit L. Hall, *The Rights of the
Accused: The Justices and Criminal Jus-
tice.* New York and London:
Garland/Taylor & Francis, 2000.

7 Sally E. Hadden, *Slave Patrols: Law and
Violence in Virginia and the Carolinas.*
Cambridge, MA: Harvard University
Press, 2001.

8 U.S. Constitution, Amendment XIV.

9 *Yick Wo* v. *Hopkins*, 118 U.S. 356 (1886)

10 *Shaughnessy* v. *Mezei*, 345 U.S. 206
(1953); *Plyler* v. *Doe* 457 U.S. 202
(1982); *U.S.* v. *Verdugo-Urquidez*, 494
U.S. 259 (1990).

11 *Boyd* v. *U.S.* 116 U.S. 616 (1886); *Weeks*
v. *United States*, 232 U.S. 383 (1914);
Paul L. Murphy, *World War I and the
Origin of Civil Liberties in the United
States.* New York: W.W. Norton & Co,
1979; *Brown* v. *State of Mississippi*, 297
U.S. 278 (1936).

12 *Powell* v. *Alabama*, 287 U.S. 45 (1932);
Norris v. *Alabama*, 294 U.S. 587 (1935).

13 *Mapp* v. *Ohio*, 367 U.S. 643 (1961); *Weeks* v.
United States, 232 U.S. 383 (1914).

14 *Gideon* v. *Wainwright*, 372 U.S. 335 (1963).

15 *Miranda* v. *Arizona*, 384 U.S. 436
(1966).

16 U.S. Constitution, Amendments XVIII
and XXI; John Kobler, *Ardent Spirits:
The Rise and Fall of Prohibition.*
London: Michael Joseph, Ltd., 1973.

17 *Katz* v. *U.S.*, 389 U.S. 347 (1967).

18 Wayne R. LaFave, *Search and Seizure:
A Treatise on the Fourth Amendment*,
3rd ed., vol. 1. St. Paul, MN: West
Publishing Co., 1996, pp. 383–384;
18 USC 2510–2520.

19 Anthony Lewis, *Gideon's Trumpet.*
New York: Random House Vintage, 1964.

20 *Mapp* v. *Ohio*; Potter Stewart, "The
Road to *Mapp* v. *Ohio* and Beyond:
The Origins, Development and Future
of the Exclusionary Rule in Search-and-
Seizure Cases," 83 COLUM. L. REV. 1365,
1367 (1983); *Miranda* v. *Arizona* 384
U.S. at 492, 516; *Katz* v. *U.S.*, 389 U.S.
347 (1967).

21 *Terry* v. *Ohio*, 392 U.S. 1 (1968).

22 *Wong Sun* v. *U.S.*, 371 U.S. 471 (1963);
U.S. v. *Sokolow*, 490 U.S. 1 (1989).

Point: "Technicalities" in Criminal Trials Protect Everybody's Freedoms

23 *Mapp* v. *Ohio*, 367 U.S. 643; Samuel Dash,
*The Intruders: Unreasonable Searches
and Seizures from King John to John
Ashcroft.* New Brunswick, NJ: Rutgers
University Press, 2004, pp. 93–95.

24 *Papachristou* v. *City of Jacksonville*, 405 U.S. 156 (1972).

25 Jerome Skolnick, *Justice Without Trial: Law Enforcement in a Democratic Society*, 3rd ed. New York: MacMillan, 1994, p. 271.

26 Francis A. Allen, "The Judicial Quest for Penal Justice: The Warren Court and the Criminal Cases," LAW FORUM, vol. 1975, No. 4, 518, 539; reprinted in Kermit L. Hall, ed., *The Rights of the Accused: The Justices and Criminal Justice*, New York and London: Garland/Taylor & Francis, 2000.

27 Ibid., p. 523.

28 Skolnick, *Justice Without Trial*, p. 281, quoting Steven Wisotsky, "Crackdown: The Emerging 'Drug Exception' to the Bill of Rights," 38 HASTINGS L.J. 889, (1987).

29 392 U.S. 1 (1968).

30 *U.S.* v. *Watson*, 423 U.S. 411 (1976); *Atwater* v. *City of Lago Vista*, 532 U.S. 318 (2001); LaFave, *Search and Seizure*, vol. 3, sec. 5.1(b), pp. 12–16 and 2003 pocket part for Sec. 5.1(b).

31 *U.S.* v. *Place*, 462 U.S. 696 (1983); *Florida* v. *Riley*, 488 U.S. 445 (1989); *Kyllo* v. *U.S.*, 533 U.S. 27 (2001); *California* v. *Greenwood*, 486 U.S. 35 (1988); *U.S.* v. *Lee*, 274 U.S. 559 (1927); LaFave, *Search and Seizure*, vol. 1, sec. 2.2(b)–(d), pp. 407–431, sec. 2.6(c), pp. 589–604, and corresponding 2003 pocket parts; Skolnick, *Justice Without Trial*, pp. 281–282.

32 *Florida* v. *Bostick*, 501 U.S. 429 (1991); Skolnick, *Justice Without Trial*, p. 283.

33 *Matlock* v. *United States*, 415 U.S. 164 (1974); *Illinois* v. *Rodriguez*, 497 U.S. 177 (1990).

34 *Camara* v. *Municipal Court*, 387 U.S. 523 (1967); *Wyman* v. *James*, 400 U.S. 309 (1971).

35 *California* v. *Carney*, 471 U.S. 386 (1985).

36 *Payton* v. *New York*, 445 U.S. 573 (1980); LaFave, *Search and Seizure*, vol. 3, sec. 6.1(a)–(b) pp. 226–233.

37 *Minnesota* v. *Olson*, 495 U.S. 91 (1990); *Vale* v. *Louisiana*, 399 U.S. 30 (1970); *Welsh* v. *Wisconsin*, 466 U.S. 740 (1984).

38 *Steagald* v. *U.S.*, 451 U.S. 204 (1979).

39 *Chimel* v. *California*, 395 U.S. 752 (1969).

40 *U.S.* v. *King*, 227 F.3d 732 (6th Cir. 2000).

41 *United States* v. *Alexander*, 761 F.2d 1294 (9th Cir. 1985).

42 *Horton* v. *California*, 496 U.S. 128 (1990).

43 Michael D. Granston, "Note: From Private Places to Private Activities: Toward a New Fourth Amendment House for the Shelterless," 101 YALE L.J. 1305 (1992).

44 *U.S.* v. *Santana*, 427 U.S. 38 (1976).

45 *State* v. *Morse*, 125 N.H. 403, 480 A.2d 183 (1984).

46 LaFave, *Search and Seizure*, vol. 3, sec. 6.1(e), pp. 255–256.

47 Jon M. Van Dyke and Melvin M. Sakurai, *Checklists for Searches and Seizures in Public Schools*. St. Paul, MN: West Group, 2004; *New Jersey* v. *T.L.O.*, 469 U.S. 325 (1985).

48 *Coolidge* v. *New Hampshire*, 403 U.S. 443, 458 (1971).

49 *New York* v. *Belton*, 453 U.S. 454 (1981).

50 Note, Kendra Hillman Chilcoat, "The Automobile Exception Swallows the Rule, *Florida* v. *White*," 90 J. CRIM. L. & CRIMINOLOGY 917, Northwestern University School of Law, 2000; *Pennsylvania* v. *Labron*, 518 U.S. 938 (1996).

51 *California* v. *Acevedo*, 500 U.S. 565 (1991).

52 *Wyoming* v. *Houghton*, 526 U.S. 295 (1999).

53 *South Dakota* v. *Opperman*, 428 U.S. 364 (1976).

54 *Florida* v. *White*, 526 U.S. 559 (1999); Chilcoat, "The Automobile Exception Swallows the Rule."

55 *Austin* v. *U.S.*, 509 U.S. 602 (1993).

56 *United States* v. *Ursery*, 518 U.S. 267 (1996).

57 See, e.g., Steven Duke, "The Drug War on the Constitution," Cato Institute. *http://www.cato.org/realaudio/drug-war/papers/duke.html.*

58 *Caplin & Drysdale, Chartered* v. *United States,* 491 U.S. 617 (1989).

59 Andrew Schneider and Mary Pat Flaherty, series, "Presumed Guilty," August 11–16, 1991, *The Pittsburgh Press,* copyright *The Pittsburgh Post-Gazette*: "Government Seizures Victimize Innocent," August 11, 1991.

60 Cary H. Copeland, "Justice Dept. Replies to 'Guilty' Series," September 1, 1991, *The Pittsburgh Press,* copyright *The Pittsburgh Post-Gazette.*

61 *Miranda* v. *Arizona,* 384 U.S. at 467–474.

62 See, e.g., *Berkemer* v. *McCarty,* 468 U.S. 420 (1984).

63 *Hiibel* v. *Sixth Judicial District Court of Nevada,* Humboldt County, Docket No. 03-5554, 124 S. Ct. 2451 (2004).

64 *Fellers* v. *United States,* Docket No. 02-6320, 124 S.Ct. 1019 (2004); *Chavez* v. *Martinez,* 538 U.S. 760 (2003); *Missouri* v. *Seibert,* Docket No. 02-1371, 124 S.Ct. 2601 (2004); *United States* v. *Patane,* Docket No. 02-1183, 124 S. Ct., 2620 (2004).

Counterpoint: Too Much Concern for Formal Rights Interferes With Crime Fighting

65 *Miranda,* Harlan dissent, 384 U.S. at 518-519.

66 Roger J. Traynor, "The Devils of Due Process in Criminal Detection, Detention, and Trial," *The Benjamin N. Cardozo Memorial Lectures; Delivered Before the Association of the Bar of the City of New York 1941–1970,* 100th Anniversary Edition, vol. 2. New York: Matthew Bender, pp. 854–855.

67 *Dirty Harry,* Dir., Don Siegel, Warner Studios, 1971.

68 Joseph Wambaugh, *The Onion Field.* New York: Dell Publishing, 1973; reprinted Delacorte Press, New York, 1979, p. 408.

69 Skolnick, *Justice Without Trial,* pp. 244–245.

70 *U.S.* v. *Calandra,* 414 U.S. 338 (1974); *U.S.* v. *Leon,* 468 U.S. 897 (1984); Christopher Slobogin, *Criminal Procedure: Regulation of Police Investigation: Legal, Historical, Empirical and Comparative Materials.* The Michie Company, 1993, pp. 495–497; *Mapp* v. *Ohio; Stone* v. *Powell,* 428 U.S. 465 (1976); Stewart, The Road to *Mapp* v. *Ohio,* pp. 1389–1392, citing, e.g., *Alderman* v. *U.S.,* 394 U.S. 165 (1969); *U.S.* v. *Havens,* 446 U.S. 620 (1980).

71 *Nix* v. *Williams,* 467 U.S. 431, 443 (1984); *Murray* v. *United States,* 487 U.S. 533 (1988), and see Louis Michael Seidman, "Akhil Amar and the (Premature?) Demise of Criminal Procedure Liberalism," book review, 107 YALE L. J. 2281, 2299, 1998.

72 See *California* v. *Acevedo,* 500 U.S. 565, 581 (1991); *City of West Covina* v. *Perkins,* 525 U.S. 234 (1999), concurrence, Thomas and Scalia.

73 Akhil Reed Amar, "Fourth Amendment First Principles," 107 HARV. L. REV. 757, 758, 797 and *passim* (1994), and see note 2 above.

74 Paul G. Cassell and Richard Fowles, "Handcuffing the Cops? A Thirty-Year Perspective on Miranda's Harmful Effects on Law Enforcement," 50 STAN. L. REV. 1055 (1998). Available at *http://www.law.utah.edu/faculty/websites/cassellp/STANFIN.html.*

75 John J. Donohue III, "Did *Miranda* Diminish Police Effectiveness?" 50 Stanford L.J. 1147, 1149 (April 1998).

76 18 U.S. Code, Chapter 119.

77 Title 42 U.S. Code, Chapter 46.

78 *Dickerson* v. *U.S.,* 530 U.S. 428 (2000), fn. 7; "Time to Overhaul Miranda?," Cassell's Website, *http://www.law.utah.edu/faculty/websites/cassellp/main5.html.*

Point: "Profiling" Makes Prejudice Official

79 "Racial Profiling Within Law Enforcement Agencies," Hearing before the

Subcommittee on the Constitution, Federalism, and Property Rights, Committee on the Judiciary, United States Senate, Sen. Hearing No. 106-996, Serial No. J-106-74. Washington, D.C.: U.S. Government Printing Office, 2001, Available at *http://www.access.gpo.gov/ congress/*, specifically *http://frwebgate.access.gpo.gov/cgi-bin/ getdoc.cgi?dbname=106_senate_hearings &docid=f:72780.pdf*, testimony of Master Sergeant Rossano Gerald, pp. 11–15.

80 Jake Tapper, "Fade to White: The only African American Republican in Congress is headed home. Can the party of Lincoln—and Trent Lott—afford the loss of J.C. Watts?" *Washington Post*, January 5, 2003, p. W6. Available at *http://www.washingtonpost.com/ wp-dyn/articles/A2933-2003Jan2.html*.

81 Paul Farhi and Linton Weeks, "With the Sniper, TV Profilers Missed Their Mark," *Washington Post*, October 25, 2002, p. C01. Available at *http://www .washingtonpost.com/wp-dyn/ articles/A13761-2002Oct24.html*.

82 Ibid.; Alan Cooper, "Muhammad influence over Malvo at issue," *Richmond Times-Dispatch*, November 3, 2004. Available at *http://www.timesdispatch .com/servlet/Satellite?pagename=RTD%2 FMGArticle%2FRTD_BasicArticle&c=M GArticle&cid=1031778912604&path=!ne ws&s=1045855934842*; Matthew Barakat, "Malvo admits 2002 sniper killing, gets life without parole," Associated Press, syndicated in the *San Francisco Chronicle*, October 26, 2004. Available at *http://www.sfgate .com/cgi-bin/article.cgi?file=/news/ archive/2004/10/26/national1853EDT071 4.DTL*.

83 Deborah Ramirez, Jack McDevitt, and Amy Farrell, "A Resource Guide on Racial Profiling Data Collection Systems: Promising Practices and Lessons Learned," U.S. Department of Justice, NCJ 184768, November 2000, FN 33. Available at *http://www.ncjrs.org/pdf-files1/bja/184768.pdf*, citing further to Randall Kennedy, *Race, Crime and the Law*, New York: Pantheon Books, 1997.

84 Cesare Lombroso, *Crime: Its Causes and Remedies*, Trans. Henry P. Horton, introduction by Maurice Parmelee. Boston: Little, Brown, & Co., 1911; reprinted by Patterson Smith Publishing, Montclair, NJ, 1968.

85 Richard F. Wetzell, *Inventing the Criminal: A History of German Criminology, 1880–1945*. Chapel Hill and London: University of North Carolina Press, 2000, pp. 301–302.

86 "Who do we think we are?" *The London Observer*, Sunday January 13, 2002, Available at *http://www.guardian.co.uk/ Archive/Article/0,4273,4334189,00.html*; Barbara Tuchman, *The Proud Tower: A Portrait of the World Before the War, 1890–1914*. New York: Macmillan Co., 1966, pp. 171–226.

87 Louis F. Post, *The Deportations Delirium of Nineteen-Twenty: A Personal Narrative of an Historic Official Experience*. Chicago: Charles H. Kerr & Co., 1923. Reprinted New York: Da Capo Press 1970, pp. 18–26.

88 Roger Daniels, *Concentration Camps: North America: Japanese in the United States and Canada during World War II*. Krieger Publishing Co., 1993.

89 Gary Stewart, "Black Codes and Broken Windows: The Legacy of Racial Hegemony in Anti-Gang Civil Injunctions," 107 YALE L. REV. 2249, 2260–2261 (1998).

90 Adam Liptak, "Pardon for 35 arrested in '99: Case in Texas largely made by agent indicted now for perjury," *New York Times*, syndicated in *San Francisco Chronicle*, August 23, 2003. *http://sfgate .com/cgi-bin/article.cgi?file=/chronicle/ archive/2003/08/23/MN243996.DTL*.

91 *S. 989: The End Racial Profiling Act of 2001*, hearing before the U.S. Senate Judiciary Subcommittee on the Constitution, Federalism and Property Rights, S. Hrg. No. 107-537, August 1, 2001, p. 124. Available at *http://www .gpoaccess.gov*, specifically *http://frwebgate.access.gpo.gov/cgi-bin/getdoc.cgi? dbname=107_senate_hearings&docid= f:80475.pdf*; David A. Harris, *Profiles in*

Injustice: Why Racial Profiling Cannot Work. New York: W.W. Norton & Co, 2002, p. 109.

92 Tracy Wood and Faye Fiore, "Beating Victim Says He Obeyed Police," *Los Angeles Times,* March 7, 1991, p. A1, cited in testimony of Robert P. Mosteller, Senate Judiciary Committee Hearing No. 106-269, *A Proposed Constitutional Amendment to Protect Crime Victims,* 1999, p. 242, n. 40. Available online at *www.access.gpo.gov/congress/.*

93 New York Attorney General Eliot Spitzer, "The New York City Police Department's 'Stop & Frisk' Practices," Civil Rights Bureau, Attorney General of the State of New York, December 1, 1999, p. 5. Available at h*ttp://www.oag .state.ny.us/press/reports/stop_frisk/ stop_frisk.html.*

94 *S. 989* hearing, pp. 60–62, 83–84 112–114.

95 Harris, *Profiles in Injustice,* pp. 195–201; and see "The Benefits of Audio-Visual Technology In Addressing Racial Profiling," Hearing, House Committee on Government Reform, July 19, 2001, No. 107-36.

96 *S. 989* hearing, submission for the record, David Cole and John Lamberth, "The Fallacy of Racial Profiling," *The New York Times,* May 13, 2001, reprinted at page 93.

97 Spitzer study, pp. vii, ix.

98 *Racial Profiling* hearing; *S.989* hearing.

99 *Newsweek,* "The Latest Trouble with Racial Profiling," January 14, 2002, p. 8.

100 "U.S. Customs Service Passenger Inspection Operations," Hearing, House Ways and Means Committee, Subcommittee on Oversight, Serial No. 106-45, May 20, 1999, pp. 28–29, Available online at *http://www.access.gpo.gov/ congress/.*

101 Ibid. pp. 2, 6–7.

102 *S. 989* hearing, remarks of Senator Richard J. Durbin, D.-IL, p. 10; testimony of ex-Commissioner Kelly, pp. 38–42.

103 S.2132; H.R. 3847, 108th Congress, introduced February 26, 2004. See *thomas.loc.gov.*

104 Rachel King, "Memo in Opposition of S. 254, the Violent and Repeat Juvenile Offender Accountability and Rehabilitation Act of 1999," ACLU, March 10, 1999. Available at *http://www.aclu.org/ CriminalJustice/CriminalJustice.cfm?ID= 5019&c=46;* Lorenza Munoz, "Gang Listing Questioned by Rights Groups," *Los Angeles Times,* July 14, 1997; Harris, *Profiles in Injustice,* pp. 6–7, 136–139.

105 Deirdre McNamer, "Checking It Twice Dept.: Here's Johnnie," *The New Yorker,* May 13, 2002. Available at *http://www .newyorker.com/printable/?talk/020513ta_ talk_mcnamer.*

106 Lisa Friedman, "David Nelsons Want Off The List," *Los Angeles Daily News,* June 15, 2003; "Report: Terror System Flags David Nelsons," Associated Press, June 15, 2003, see, e.g., *http://www .newsday.com/news/nationworld/nation/ wire/sns-ap-nelson-flight-list,0,28101 .story?coll=sns-ap-nation-headlines.*

107 Alan Gathright, "ACLU Seeks Answers On 'No-Fly' Lists: It seeks criteria used to identify a passenger as potential threat," *San Francisco Chronicle,* December 13, 2002, p. A25.

108 James Sterngold, "Iranians furious over INS arrests: Abuse alleged after men agreed to register in L.A.," *San Francisco Chronicle,* December 21, 2002; George Lardner, Jr., "Brookings Scholar is Detained by INS: Registration Rule Snags Pakistani Editor," *Washington Post,* January 30, 2003, p. A1; "U.S. Detains Nearly 1,200 During Registry," *Washington Post,* January 17, 2003, p. A14.

109 *www.aclu.org,* "Safe and Free—Detention" Web page, *http://www.aclu.org/ SafeandFree/SafeandFree.cfm?ID=13079 &c=207.*

Counterpoint: Profiling and Prejudice Are Different

110 Milagros Cisneros, "H.B. 2659: Notorious Notaries—How Arizona is Curbing *Notario* Fraud in the Immigrant Community." 32 ARIZ. ST. L.J. 287 (Spr. 2000).

111 David McGuire, "Military, Private Sector Rush to Adopt High-Tech Security Technology," Washingtonpost.com, September 24, 2002, Available at *http://www.washingtonpost.com/wp-dyn/ articles/A56706-2002Sep23.html.*

112 *U.S. Customs Service* . . . hearing, pp. 24–25, 27, 29.

113 Ibid., p. 25.

114 *S989* hearing, Statement of Raymond W. Kelly, pp. 38–40.

115 Robert O'Harrow, Jr., "Air Security Focusing on Flier Screening," *Washington Post*, September 4, 2002. Available at *http://www.washingtonpost.com/ac2/ wp-dyn/A34738-2002Sep3?language =printer*; Admiral James M. Loy, Foreign Press Center Briefing, Washington D.C., August 26, 2003, State Department transcript, available at *http://fpc.state.gov/ 23542.htm.*

116 ACLU press release, March 25, 2003, "Right-Left Groups Tell Homeland Security Committee to Curb CAPPS II," available at *http://www.aclu.org/Safe-andFree/SafeandFree.cfm?ID=12173&c= 206.*

117 Richard Lowry, "Profiles in Cowardice: How to deal with the terrorist threat— and how not to," *National Review Online*, January 28, 2002. Available at *http://www.nationalreview.com/flash-back/flashback-lowryprint030402.html.*

118 *Terry* v. *Ohio*, 392 U.S. 1, 21 (1968).

119 Heather Mac Donald, *Are Cops Racist?* Chicago: Ivan R. Dee, 2003, p. 145.

120 *Racial Profiling* hearing, testimony of Johnny L. Hughes, National Troopers Coalition, p. 42.

121 William Tucker, "The Tragedy of Racial Profiling: It's Unjust—And It Works," *Weekly Standard*, June 18, 2001, quoted in *S989* hearing record, pp. 125–129.

122 "Criminal Victimization in United States, 1999 Statistical Tables, National Crime Victimization Survey," U.S. Department of Justice, Bureau of Justice Statistics, January 2001, Table 40, p. 43. Available at *http://www.ojp.usdoj.gov/ bjs/pub/pdf/cvus99.pdf.*

123 Compare Spitzer study, pp. vii and ix of the executive summary and tables cited therein.

124 *S989* hearing, testimony of Police Chief Reuben Greenberg of Charleston, SC, pp. 75–76.

125 *S989* hearing, testimony of Steve Young, National Vice President, Fraternal Order of Police, p. 32.

126 Sharon Turco and Jane Prendergast, "Crime's up and arrests down: Officials beginning to discuss slowdown by police," *The Cincinnati Enquirer*, January 30, 2003. Available at *http://www.enquirer.com/editions/ 2003/01/30/loc_slowdown30.html.*

127 Vernon Loeb, "Clan, family ties called key to Army's capture of Hussein: 'Link Diagrams' showed everyone related by blood or tribe." *Washington Post*, December 16, 2003, p. A27. Available at *http://www.washingtonpost.com/ac2/ wp-dyn/A3075-2003Dec15?language =printer.*

128 Raymond Dussault, "CAL/GANG Brings Dividends," *Government Technology*, December 1998. Available at *http://www.govtech.net/magazine/ gt/1998/dec/jandt/jandt.phtml.*

129 Leslie Miller, "Government orders airlines to turn over passenger data," Associated Press, syndicated in the *Detroit Free Press*, November 12, 2004. Available at *http://www.freep.com/news/latest-news/pm1342_20041112.htm.*

130 Suzanne Herel and Tyche Hendricks, "Fremont police turn down ACLU, will help FBI with questioning," *San Francisco Chronicle*, December 5, 2001, online edition, available at *http://sfgate.com/ cgibin/article.cgi?file=/chronicle/ archive/2001/12/05/MN146287. DTL*; Suzanne Herel, "Police leery of U.S. probe: Bay Area nonimmigrant visa holders face questioning," *San Francisco Chronicle*, December 4, 2001, online edition, available at *http://sfgate.com/cgi-bin/article .cgi?file=/chronicle/archive/2001/12/ 04/MN11934.DTL.*

131 Steven Brill, "The FBI Gets Religion: It could have been a disaster. But the bureau's dragnet of young Middle Eastern men went better than anyone expected," *Newsweek*, January 28, 2002.

Point: Existing Legal Protections Are Not Stopping Unfair Policing

132 *Koon* v. *U.S.*, 518 U.S. 81 (1996); Richard Serrano, "Police Documents Disclose Beating was Downplayed . . . " *Los Angeles Times*, March 20, 1991, p. A1; Cecelia Rasmussen, "The Rodney King Case Chronology: The Police Beating of King has Triggered the Following Events," *Los Angeles Times*, July 10, 1991, p. A12.

133 *Terry* v. *Ohio*, 392 U.S. 1, 13-15 (1968).

134 *Chavez* v. *Martinez*, 538 U.S. 760 (2003).

135 Harris, *Profiles in Injustice*, pp. 87–89.

136 Author's experience, primarily San Francisco, CA.

137 *Mathews* v. *Eldridge*, 424 U.S 319 (1976).

138 John Mitchell, "Punitive Damages from Police in King Beating Rejected," *Los Angeles Times*, June 2, 1994, P. A1; Ted Rohrlich, "Rodney King in Legal Quagmire," *Los Angeles Times*, August 16, 2000, p. B1.

139 *Monroe* v. *Pape*, 365 U.S. 167 (1961); *Monell* v. *Dept. of Social Services*, 436 U.S. 658 (1978); Rodney A. Smolla, *Federal Civil Rights Acts*, 3rd Ed., vol. 2. West Group, 2001, sec. 14:1–3; Erwin Chemerinsky, *Federal Jurisdiction*. Aspen Publishers, 2003, Secs. 8.2–8.5, pp. 469–492; *Bivens* v. *Six Unknown Named Agents of the Federal Bureau of Narcotics*, 403 U.S. 388 (1971); Smolla, sec. 14:149–150.

140 Chemerinsky, *Federal Jurisdiction*, sec. 8.3, p. 477; *Lugar* v. *Edmondson Oil Co.*, 457 U.S. 922 (1982).

141 Prison Litigation Reform Act, Pub. Law No. 104-134. See Chemerinsky, *Federal Jurisdiction*, Sec. 8.1, p. 467.

142 *Edelman* v. *Jordan*, 415 U.S. 651 (1974); *Quern* v. *Jordan*, 440 U.S. 332 (1979); *Will* v. *Michigan Department of State Police*, 491 U.S. 58 (1989); Chemerinsky, *Federal Jurisdiction*, sec. 8.7, pp. 540–541.

143 Chemerinsky, *Federal Jurisdiction*, sec. 8.5, pp. 506–509.

144 Chemerinsky, *Federal Jurisdiction*, sec. 8.6, pp. 516–528; *Briscoe* v. *LaHue*, 460 U.S. 325 (1983).

145 Re: school officials, see *Wood* v. *Strickland*, 420 U.S. 308 (1975); Chemerinsky, *Federal Jurisdiction*, p. 530.

146 *Saucier* v. *Katz*, 533 U.S. 194 (2001)

147 Chemerinsky, *Federal Jurisdiction*, p. 540; *Richardson* v. *McKnight*, 521 U.S. 399 (1997).

148 18 U.S. Code §§ 241, 242.

149 Richard Serrano, Tracy Wilkinson, "All 4 in King Beating Acquitted; Violence follows verdicts; Guard called out . . . " *Los Angeles Times*, April 30, 1992, p. A1.

150 Opinion, "Curtain Closes on the King Case: with Final Court Ruling Made, Ex-Sgt. Koon is Free—and Rich." *Los Angeles Times*, September 30, 1996, p. B4; *Koon* v. *United States*, 518 U.S. 81 (1996).

151 45 CFR Chapter XVI.

152 *Rizzo* v. *Goode*, 423 U.S. 387 (1976); Slobogin, *Criminal Procedure:* pp. 513–515.

153 Transcript, CNN Saturday Morning News, "Are Cincinnati Police Guilty of Racial Profiling?" April 14, 2001. Available at *http://transcripts.cnn.com/ TRANSCRIPTS/0104/14/smn.08.html*; Turco and Prendergast, "Crime's up", *http://www.enquirer.com/editions/ 2003/01/30/loc_slowdown30.html*; *Bomani Tyehimba* v. *City of Cincinnati*, Case No. C-1-99-317; *In Re Cincinnati Policing*, Case No. C-1-99-3170, U.S. Dist. Court, Southern Dist. of Ohio, Western Div.

154 Skolnick, *Justice Without Trial*, pp. 112–113, 199–205.

155 James W. Williams, "Taking it the Streets: Policing and the Practice of Constitutive Criminology," in *Constitutive*

Criminology at Work: Applications to Crime and Justice, Ed. Stuart Henry and Dragan Milovanovic. Albany: State University of New York Press, 1999, pp. 154–157.

156 James Q. Wilson and George L. Kelling, "Broken Windows: The Police and Neighborhood Safety," *Atlantic Monthly,* March 1982.

157 *Atwater* v. *City of Lago Vista,* 532 U.S. 318 (2001).

158 *Whren* v. *U.S.,* 517 U.S. 806 (1996).

159 *Shuttlesworth* v. *City of Birmingham,* 382 U.S. 87 (1965); *Papachristou* v. *City of Jacksonville,* 405 U.S. 156 (1972); *Kolender* v. *Lawson,* 461 U.S. 352 (1983).

160 *Powell* v. *Texas,* 392 U.S. 514 (1968).

161 Stewart, "Black Codes."

162 Ibid.; Christian Parenti, *Lockdown America: Police and Prisons in the Age of Crisis.* London and New York: Verso, 1999, pp. 120–123.

163 William Bratton, "Cutting Crime and Restoring Order: What America Can Learn from New York's Finest," transcript, The Heritage Foundation, October 15, 1996, Heritage Lecture No. 573.

164 Harris, *Profiles in Injustice,* p. 43; *Minnesota* v. *Dickerson;* 508 U.S. 366 (1993); *Illinois* v. *Wardlow,* 528 U.S. 119 (2000).

165 Spitzer study, Chapter 5.

166 Sara Rimer, "Unruly Students Facing Arrest, Not Detention," *New York Times,* January 4, 2004. Available at *http://www .nytimes.com/2004/01/04/education/ 04TOLE.html?ex=1084852800&en =f67df2b2893153b4&ei=5070.*

167 Heather Knight, "Board votes for counselors over cops," *San Francisco Chronicle,* May 29, 2003. Available at *http://www.sfgate.com/cgi-bin/article .cgi?file=/chronicle/archive/2003/05/29/B A302434.DTL;* Ray Delgado, "S.F. High School reopens after melee; Marshall parents confront officials," *San Francisco Chronicle,* October 16, 2002. Available at *http://www.sfgate.com/cgi-bin/article .cgi?file=/chronicle/archive/2002/10/16/B A93934.DTL.*

168 Harris, *Profiles in Injustice,* pp. 127–128.

169 Judith A. Greene, "Zero Tolerance: A Case Study of Police Policies and Practices in New York City," 45 CRIME & DELINQUENCY 2, April 1999, 171, 174, 176, 183–185, fn. 6.

170 See "Legislation Related to the Attack of September 11, 2001," THOMAS, available at *http://thomas.loc.gov/ home/terrorleg.htm.*

171 "Report of the Senate Select Committee to Study Governmental Operations With Respect to Intelligence Activities," 94th Cong., 2d Sess., Report No. 94-755 (1976) ("Church Committee Report"); "The Dangers of Domestic Spying by Federal Law Enforcement: A Case Study on FBI Surveillance of Dr. Martin Luther King," available from the ACLU at *http://www.aclu.org/Files/ Files.cfm?ID=9999&c=184>.;* Chris Mooney, "Back to Church," *The American Prospect,* November 5, 2001. Available at *http://www.prospect.org/print/ V12/19/mooney-c.html.*

172 "The "Carnivore" Controversy: Electronic Surveillance and Privacy in the Digital Age," Hearing, Sen. Judiciary Committee, 106th Cong., 2nd Sess., Sen. Hrg. No. 106-1057, September 6, 2000. Available at *http://www.access .gpo.gov/congress/.*

173 ACLU legislative analysis, USA PATRIOT Act, November 1, 2001. FISA, 50 USC 1801 et seq.; USA PATRIOT Act, P.L. No. 107-56, Sec. 218.

174 Anne Gearan, Associated Press, "Supreme court rejects attempt to appeal cases testing scope of secret spy court," *San Francisco Chronicle,* March 24, 2003. Available at *http://www.sfgate.com/cgi- bin/article.cgi?file=/news/archive/2003/03/ 24/national1009EST0602.DTL.*

175 "Criminal, Intelligence Agents Work Side by Side in Terror Cases," Dan Eggen, *Washington Post,* syndicated in *San Francisco Chronicle,* December 13, 2003. Available at *http://sfgate.com/ cgi-bin/article.cgi?file=/chronicle/ archive/2003/12/13/MNGFB3MO9M1 .DTL.*

176 ACLU study on domestic spying, available at *http://www.aclu.org/files/files.cfm ?ID=9999&c=184.*

177 USA PATRIOT Act, Sec. 501.

178 Homeland Security Act, Pub. Law No. 107-296, Secs. 201-215; "Fact Sheet: Strengthening Intelligence to Better Protect America," released January 28, 2003; The White House, available at *http://www.whitehouse.gov/news/releases/ 2003/01/20030128-12.html.*

179 *Hamdi* v. *Rumsfeld,* 03-6696, 124 S.Ct. 2633 (2004); *Rumsfeld* v. *Padilla,* 03-1027, 124 S. Ct. 2711 (2004); and *Rasul* v. *Bush,* 03-334 and 03-343, 124 S. Ct. 2686 (2004); Ronald Dworkin, "What The Court Really Said," *New York Review of Books,* August 12, 2004. Available at *http://www.nybooks.com/ articles/17293.*

180 See, e.g., Neil A. Lewis, "Red Cross Finds Detainee Abuse in Guantánamo," *New York Times,* November 30, 2004.

181 See, e.g. HR. 10, S. 2845, 108th Congress, bill texts and histories available at *http://thomas.loc.gov/* and via the *Congressional Record.*

Counterpoint: Restricting Search and Seizure Power Too Much Hurts Public Safety

182 Catherine Coles and George Kelling, "Q: Is the rigorous enforcement of anti-nuisance laws a good idea?" *Insight,* The Manhattan Institute, June 2, 1997. Available at *http://www.manhattan-institute.org/html/_insight-is_the_ rigorous.htm.*

183 "The Boyd Booth Story: A Community Takes Charge," The Community Law Center, Baltimore, MD. *http://www .communitylaw.org/Boyd%20Booth%20S tory.htm;* Jeffrey Roth, George Kelling, "Baltimore's Comprehensive Communities Program: A Case Study," prepared for the National Institute of Justice by BOTEC Analysis Corporation, March 25, 2004. Available at *http://www.ncjrs.org/ pdffiles1/nij/grants/204627.pdf.*

184 Skolnick, *Justice Without Trial,* pp. 16–17.

185 Philip Matier and Andrew Ross, "Cops' guns no match for gang-bangers' AK-47s," *San Francisco Chronicle,* April 26, 2004. Available at *http://www.sfgate.com/ cgi-bin/article.cgi?file=/chronicle/ archive/2004/04/26/BAG4R6B18P1.DTL.*

186 Quoted in review by Ted Conover, *The New York Times,* April 18, 2004, from Edward Conlon, *Blue Blood.* New York: Riverhead Books, 2004. Available at *http://query.nytimes.com/gst/fullpage .html?res=9C02E4DF1538F93BA25757C 0A9629C8B63.*

187 S989 hrg; Hatch remarks, p. 7; Gregory Korte, "DeWine attacks police slow-down: Says Luken should be more demanding of officers," *The Cincinnati Enquirer,* February 1, 2003. Available at *http://www.enquirer.com/editions/ 2003/02/01/loc_dewine01.html.*

188 Mac Donald, *Are Cops Racist?,* p. 84

189 Arthur M. Schlesinger, Jr., *Robert Kennedy and His Times.* Boston: Houghton Mifflin Co., 1978, pp. 166–169, 281–285.

190 John Ashcroft, prepared remarks, U.S. Mayors' Conference, October 25, 2001, archived at *http://www.yale.edu/ lawweb/avalon/sept_11/doj_brief020 .htm.*

191 U.S. Department of Justice press release, "U.S. Announces Plea in Terrorism Financing Case," July 30, 2004, available at *http://www.usdoj.gov/opa/pr/2004/ July/04_crm_524.htm;* U.S. v. *Alamoudi,* U.S. District Court, Eastern District of Virginia, case Criminal No. 03-513-A, "Plea Agreement," facsimile at *http://news.findlaw.com/hdocs/docs/ terrorism/usalmdi73004plea.pdf.*

192 Edward Walsh, "One Arraigned, Two Undergo Questioning." *Washington Post,* April 22, 1995, p. A1. Available at *http://www.washingtonpost.com/ wp-srv/national/longterm/oklahoma/ stories/ok042295.htm.*

193 Bratton, Heritage Foundation lecture.

194 Bratton with Knobler, *Turnaround,* pp. 289–290.

195 *Terminiello* v. *City of Chicago,* 337 U.S. 1, 37 (1949); David Corn, "The 'Suicide

Pact' Mystery—Who coined the phrase? Justice Goldberg or Justice Jackson?" *Slate Magazine*, January 4, 2002. Available at *http://slate.msn.com/ id/2060342/*.

196 Jonathan Alter, "Time to Think About Torture," *Newsweek*, November 5, 2001.

197 "Webcams enforce SARS quarantine," Reuters via MSNBC, April 10, 2003.

198 *Ex Parte Quirin*, 317 U.S. 1 (1942).

199 Tom Jackman, "U.S. Can Hold Citizens as Enemy Combatants: Appeals Court Rules in Favor of Government in Holding Hamdi." *Washington Post*, January 8, 2003.

200 "CIA's Inquiry on Qaeda Aide Seen as Flawed," *New York Times*, September 23, 2002; witnesses' prepared statements, U.S. Senate Select Committee on Intelligence, Joint Investigation, September 20, 2002. Available at *http://intelligence.senate.gov/0209hrg/ 020920/witness.htm*; Prepared Statement of Eleanor Hill, September 24, 2002. Available at *http://intelligence.senate.gov/ 0209hrg/020924/witness.htm*; U.S. Senate Intelligence Committee Joint Investigation witness statements, September–October 2002. Available at *http://intelligence.senate.gov/ hr107.htm*.

201 *Zurcher* v. *Stanford Daily*, 436 U.S. 547 (1978).

Conclusion

202 Joan Didion, *The White Album*. New York: Farrar, Straus & Giroux: Noonday Press, 1979.

203 Jim Herron Zamora and Meredith May, "Ex-cops cleared of 8 counts—mistrial on 27 others: Oakland Riders acquitted of misconduct charges: Deadlocked; Most jurors thought officers were scapegoats," *San Francisco Chronicle*, October 1, 2003. Available at *http://sfgate.com/cgi-bin/ article.cgi?f=/c/a/2003/10/01/MN17156. DTL*.

204 See George Orwell, "Raffles and Miss Blandish," *Horizon*, October 1944, reprinted in many essay collections and *Complete Works of George Orwell*, vol. XVI. London: Random House: Secker & Warburg, 1998, p. 345; Alexis Soloski, "Criminous Victorians," *The Believer*, October 2003, pp. 33–39.

205 Ibid.

206 Skolnick, *Justice Without Trial*, pp. vii, 241–245.

207 *Dickerson* v. *U.S.*, 530 U.S. 428 (2000), fn. 7.

208 Cassell, Website. "Time to Overhaul Miranda?," available at *http://www.law .utah.edu/faculty/websites/cassellp/ main5.html*.

209 Text on Cassell Website, available at *http://www.law.utah.edu/faculty/ websites/cassellp/fopbrief.html*.

Books

Bratton, William, with Peter Knobler. *Turnaround: How America's Top Cop Reversed the Crime Epidemic*. New York: Random House, 1998.

Chemerinsky, Erwin. *Federal Jurisdiction*. Aspen Publishers, 2003.

Collins, Michael G. *Section 1983 Litigation, In a Nutshell*, 2nd. ed. St. Paul, MN, West Group, 2001. (Note: The "Nutshell" series are study aids for lawyers and law students. They do not explore the law as carefully as treatises on the subject.)

Dash, Samuel. *The Intruders: Unreasonable Searches and Seizures from King John to John Ashcroft*. New Brunswick, NJ: Rutgers University Press, 2004.

Hadden, Sally E. *Slave Patrols: Law and Violence in Virginia and the Carolinas*, Cambridge, MA: Harvard University Press, 2001.

Harris, David A. *Profiles in Injustice: Why Racial Profiling Cannot Work*, New York: W.W. Norton & Co.: New Press, 2002.

Israel, Jerold H., Wayne R. LaFave, *Criminal Procedure: Constitutional Limitations, In a Nutshell*, 6th Ed. St. Paul, MN: West Group, 2001.

LaFave, Wayne. *Search and Seizure: A Treatise on the Fourth Amendment*, 3d Ed. St. Paul, MN: West Publishing Co., 1996.

Levy, Leonard W. *Origins of the Bill of Rights*. New Haven, CT: Yale University Press, Nota Bene, 2001.

Lewis, Anthony. *Gideon's Trumpet*. New York: Random House: Vintage, 1966. (Popularized story of prisoner Clarence Gideon's successful court battle for the right of poor criminal defendants to have lawyers at trial.)

Mac Donald, Heather. *Are Cops Racist? How the war against the police harms black Americans*. Chicago: Ivan R. Dee, 2003.

Murphy, Paul L. *World War I and the Origin of Civil Liberties in the United States*. New York: W.W. Norton & Co, 1979.

Parenti, Christian. *Lockdown America: Police and Prisons in the Age of Crisis*. London and New York: Verso, 1999.

Skolnick, Jerome H. *Justice Without Trial: Law Enforcement in Democratic Society*, 3rd ed. New York: MacMillan, 1994.

Slobogin, Christopher. *Criminal Procedure: Regulation of Police Investigation*. The Michie Co., 1993.

Van Dyke, Jon M., and Melvin M. Sakurai. *Checklists for Searches and Seizures in Public Schools*. St Paul, MN: West Group: Clark Boardman Callaghan, 2004 (updates issued annually).

Wambaugh, Joseph. *The Onion Field*. New York: Dell Publishing, 1973; reprinted Delacorte Press, New York, 1979.

Woodward, Bob, and Scott Armstrong. *The Brethren: Inside the Supreme Court*. New York: Simon & Schuster, 1979. (Popular insider history of the Supreme Court's 1969 through 1975 terms.)

Wroth, L. Kinvin, and Hiller B. Zobel, eds. *The Legal Papers of John Adams*, Cambridge, MA: Harvard University Press, Belknap Press, 1965 (Vol. 2 discusses the history of the Fourth Amendment in detail.)

Films

Becker, Harold, dir. *The Onion Field*. MGM, 1979. Based closely on Joseph Wambaugh's book, a true story about kidnapers/murderers in Los Angeles who tied up their trial for years with procedural objections.

Collins, Robert E., dir. *Gideon's Trumpet*. Republic Studios, 1980. Henry Fonda stars in the film version of Anthony Lewis's book on the Florida prisoner who established the right of poor criminal defendants to legal representation in court.

Siegel, Don, dir. *Dirty Harry*. Warner Studios, 1971. Clint Eastwood thriller that dramatizes the backlash against 1960s restrictions on police conduct.

Articles and Reports

Amar, Akhil Reed. "Fourth Amendment First Principles." 107 HARV. L. REV. 757 (1994). See also the Amar articles cited in *California* v. *Acevedo*, 500 U.S. 565 (1991).

Bratton, William. "Cutting Crime and Restoring Order: What America Can Learn from New York's Finest," transcript of lecture, The Heritage Foundation, October 15, 1996, Heritage Lecture No. 573. Available at *http://www.heritage.org/Research/Crime/HL573.cfm*.

Cassell, Paul G., and Richard Fowles. "Handcuffing the Cops? A Thirty-Year Perspective on Miranda's Harmful Effects on Law Enforcement." 50 STAN L. REV. 1055, 1059–1060 and *passim* (1998), also available at *http://www.law.utah.edu/faculty/websites/cassellp/STANFIN.html*.

"The Dangers of Domestic Spying by Federal Law Enforcement: A Case Study on FBI Surveillance of Dr. Martin Luther King," available from the ACLU at *http://www.aclu.org/Files/Files.cfm?ID=9999&c=184*.

Davies, Thomas Y. "Recovering the Original Fourth Amendment." 98 MICH. L. REV. 547 (1999). (A critique of Akhil Amar's Fourth Amendment scholarship.)

Donohue III, John J. "Did *Miranda* Diminish Police Effectiveness?" 50 STAN
L. J. 1147 (April 1998).

Maclin, Tracey. "The Central Meaning of the Fourth Amendment." 35 WM.
MARY L. REV. 197 (1993) (Another response to Akhil Amar's legal and
historical suggestions.)

"The New York City Police Department's "Stop & Frisk" Practices." Civil
Rights Bureau, Attorney General of the State of New York, December 1,
1999, available at *http://www.oag.state.ny.us/press/reports/stop_frisk/
stop_frisk.html.*

"Racial Profiling Within Law Enforcement Agencies" Hearing before
the Subcommittee on the Constitution, Federalism, and Property
Rights, Committee on the Judiciary, United States Senate, Sen. Hearing
No. 106-996. Washington, D.C.: U.S. Government Printing Office, 2001,
available at *http://www.access.gpo.gov/congress,* specifically
*http://frwebgate.access.gpo.gov/cgi-bin/getdoc.cgi?dbname=
106_senate_hearings&docid=f:72780.pdf.*

"S. 989: The End Racial Profiling Act of 2001," hearing before the U.S.
Senate Judiciary Subcommittee on the Constitution, Federalism and
Property Rights, S. Hrg. No. 107-537, August 1, 2001, available at
http://www.gpoaccess.gov/, specifically at *http://frwebgate.access
.gpo.gov/cgi-bin/getdoc.cgi?dbname=107_senate_hearings&docid
=f:80475.pdf.*

Steiker, Carol S. "Second Thoughts about First Principles." 107 HARV. L.
REV. 820 (1994). (A response to Akhil Amar's "Fourth Amendment
First Principles.")

Stewart, Gary. "Black Codes and Broken Windows." 107 YALE L. REV. 2249
(1998).

U.S. Senate Select Committee on Intelligence, Joint Investigation open
hearings, multiple dates in September and October 2002. Available
at *http://intelligence.senate.gov/hr107.htm.* (Hearings on intelligence
activities prior to the 9/11 attacks.)

Wilson, James Q., and George Kelling. "Broken Windows: The Police and
Neighborhood Safety." *The Atlantic Monthly,* March 1982. The famous
article on "Broken Windows," or "order maintenance," policing.

Websites

"Addressing Police Misconduct"

http://www.usdoj.gov/crt/split/documents/polmis.htm

Online brochure from the U.S. Department of Justice that explains which federal laws address police misconduct and how to file a federal complaint.

The American Civil Liberties Union (ACLU)

http://www.aclu.org

The Website of the large liberal and civil-libertarian advocacy organization. Many sections are relevant to search and seizure issues. A special "Safe and Free" page discusses the effects of post-9/11 security measures on constitutional rights.

Cato Institute.

http://www.cato.org

Libertarian and conservative "think tank." An organization opposed to aggressive drug enforcement, civil forfeiture seizures, and other assertions of official power over the individual.

City Journal

http://www.city-journal.org

The home site of the Manhattan Institute "think tank," including Heather Mac Donald, the right-wing commentator on policing and profiling issues. Mac Donald and other contributors tend to support increased powers for U.S. police and security forces.

Cornell Legal Infomation Institute

http://lii.law.cornell.edu

A project of Cornell University Law School. Many archives of law-related materials, including unofficial texts of federal laws and Supreme Court decisions with helpful cross-linking. Use is free but the site solicits donations. (This site is a helpful research aid, but people preparing actual legal cases should check all free online materials against more official sources. See a law library reference librarian for advice.)

FindLaw

http://www.findlaw.com

A valuable, apolitical legal research site with both introductory and advanced legal commentary and unofficial texts of many laws and court decisions, including full texts of Supreme Court cases. Individual articles include one on the Fourth Amendment at *http://supreme.lp.findlaw.com/constitution/amendment04/index.html* and one on *Saucier* v. *Katz* qualified immunity issues at *http://sol.lp.findlaw.com/2000/saucier.html.* The Supreme Court cases and much other material can be browsed directly, but certain resources require free registration. (This site is a helpful research aid, but people preparing actual legal cases should check all free online materials against more official sources. See a law library reference librarian for advice.)

GPO Access

http://www.gpoaccess.gov

The Web site of the United States Government Printing Office. Offers free online access to major documents and notices from all three branches of government, including texts of many congressional hearings and reports, copies of federal laws, and many federal agencies' announcements, regulations, and requests for comment on proposed regulations.

Heritage Foundation

http://www.heritage.org

The Web site of a large conservative and right-wing "think tank." Offers policy papers on issues including biometrics, national security detentions, and conventional criminal procedure.

"Legislation Related to the Attack of September 11, 2001"

http://thomas.loc.gov/home/terrorleg.htm

A section of the Library of Congress's extensive THOMAS research database on all aspects of the United States Congress. This page lists legislative activity in Congress in response to the 2001 terrorist attack. A handy reference, especially for emergency security laws such as the USA PATRIOT Act. The main THOMAS resource page is at http://thomas.loc.gov.

National Archives and Records Administration, U.S. Constitution

http://www.archives.gov/national_archives_experience/charters/constitution_transcript.html

A transcript of the Constitution as originally written appears at this site, noting where later amendments have changed it—most notably on the abolition of slavery. Links to the Bill of Rights and the rest of the 27 amendments are available on the site.

Racial Profiling Data Collection Resource Center

http://www.racialprofilinganalysis.neu.edu

A project of the Institute on Race and Justice at Northeastern University. Many resources on racial profiling, including quick "fact sheets," news reports, legislative updates, contact and training information, and results of many profiling studies all over the United States.

"Time to Overhaul Miranda?"

http://www.law.utah.edu/faculty/websites/cassellp/main5.html

Website created by Paul Cassell, a prominent academic opponent of the *Miranda* decision who is now a federal judge.

Zimbardo Websites

http://www.zimbardo.com, http://www.prisonexp.org

Showcasing the scholarship of Philip Zimbardo, a researcher who is cited in the "Broken Windows" article and otherwise known for innovative studies of group behavior and responses to the appearance of disorder.

Cases

***Atwater* v. *City of Lago Vista*,** 532 U.S. 318 (2001)
A policeman did not break the law when he arrested a woman and took her
to jail for a seatbelt violation that would ordinarily have gotten only a ticket.
Although his behavior was unusual, it was formally "by the book." This case
supports the use of "zero-tolerance" policing to stop people for further investigation or to apply pressure to people the police otherwise think are troublemakers.

***Bivens* v. *Six Unknown Named Agents of the Federal Bureau of Narcotics*,**
403 U.S. 388 (1971)
A court-made opportunity to sue federal officials for violating constitutional
rights under color of law.

***California* v. *Acevedo*,** 500 U.S. 565 (1991)
Cites many articles on new views of Fourth Amendment history and legal theory.

***Chavez* v. *Martinez*,** 538 U.S. 760 (2003)
Upheld the behavior of a police officer who persisted in questioning a suspect
who was being treated for bullet wounds after a fight with officers. While in
fear of death, in pain, and without receiving *Miranda* warnings, the suspect was
persuaded to confess to using drugs and to his part in the fight. The Supreme
Court found his Fifth Amendment rights were not violated because he was never
prosecuted for a crime.

***Gideon* v. *Wainwright*,** 372 U.S. 335 (1963)
Criminal defendants have a right to be represented by an attorney even if they
cannot afford one.

***Katz* v. *U.S.*,** 389 U.S. 347 (1967)
The "expectation of privacy" travels with people at all times so that the Fourth
Amendment protects them in situations such as conversations on public phones
and not just when they are at home.

***Koon* v. *U.S.*,** 518 U.S. 81 (1996)
Describes the Rodney King beating and resulting court cases.

***Mapp* v. *Ohio*,** 367 U.S. 643 (1961)
Evidence obtained by an improper search may not be considered in court.

***Miranda* v. *Arizona*,** 384 U.S. 436 (1966)
Suspects who are to be questioned in a "custodial interrogation" (while held by
the police and not free to leave) must be warned of their right to remain silent
and to have an attorney present. In addition to its importance as a landmark
decision, the *Miranda* opinion text is a valuable source of Fifth Amendment
history and theory.

***Monell* v. *Department of Social Services*,** 436 U.S. 658 (1978)
Gave § 1983 plaintiffs the right to sue local (but not state) governments, not just
individual public employees. Together, *Monroe* and *Monell* made possible § 1983
lawsuits in cases like the Rodney King beating, where police claim to be enforcing
the law while in fact inflicting unlawful abuse.

Monroe v. Pape, 365 U.S. 167 (1961)

Chicago police officers broke into the Monroe family's home without a warrant, made them stand naked in the living room, tore up their beds and possessions in a search, and detained the father of the family without clear charges. The father was held without access to a lawyer and questioned about an unsolved murder. The Supreme Court found that the family could use 42 U.S. Code § 1983 to sue the policemen themselves, though not the city, for violating rights "under color of" (that is, while claiming to enforce) the state law.

Saucier v. Katz, 533 U.S. 194 (2001)

Where a plaintiff accuses an officer of excessive force, qualified immunity for purposes of a § 1983 lawsuit depends on "whether it would be clear to a reasonable officer that his conduct was unlawful in the situation he confronted."

Terry v. Ohio, 392 U.S. 1 (1968)

Authorizes the "*Terry* stop," in which police officers may stop, question, and pat-search anyone for whom they can articulate a suspicion of wrongdoing, without a warrant or a probable cause for search or arrest.

U.S. v. Montero-Camargo, 208 F.3d 1122 (9th Cir. 2000)

Detailed discussion of racial profiling and "reasonable suspicion," citing many other informative cases.

Whren v. U.S., 517 U.S. 806 (1996)

It is not a Fourth Amendment violation when police officers use a minor traffic violation as a pretext to stop someone they generically suspect of being up to no good. Officers in a high drug area noticed a man who drove away suspiciously fast after a long stop at a stop sign. The officers caught up with him, supposedly to warn him about traffic violations and in fact to check for drugs, which they did find.

Terms and Concepts

absolute immunity	order-maintenance policing
biometrics	pattern and practice
"Broken Windows" policing	pretext
class action	probable cause
color of law	profiling
crimes of status	qualified immunity
criminal profiling	racial profiling
enemy combatant	sovereign immunity
zero-tolerance policing	*Terry* stop
exclusionary rule	warrant requirement
gang databases	Warren Court
"no-fly" lists	watch lists

Beginning Legal Research

The goal of POINT/COUNTERPOINT is not only to provide the reader with an introduction to a controversial issue affecting society, but also to encourage the reader to explore the issue more fully. This appendix, then, is meant to serve as a guide to the reader in researching the current state of the law as well as exploring some of the public-policy arguments as to why existing laws should be changed or new laws are needed.

Like many types of research, legal research has become much faster and more accessible with the invention of the Internet. This appendix discusses some of the best starting points, but of course "surfing the Net" will uncover endless additional sources of information—some more reliable than others. Some important sources of law are not yet available on the Internet, but these can generally be found at the larger public and university libraries. Librarians usually are happy to point patrons in the right direction.

The most important source of law in the United States is the Constitution. Originally enacted in 1787, the Constitution outlines the structure of our federal government and sets limits on the types of laws that the federal government and state governments can pass. Through the centuries, a number of amendments have been added to or changed in the Constitution, most notably the first ten amendments, known collectively as the Bill of Rights, which guarantee important civil liberties. Each state also has its own constitution, many of which are similar to the U.S. Constitution. It is important to be familiar with the U.S. Constitution because so many of our laws are affected by its requirements. State constitutions often provide protections of individual rights that are even stronger than those set forth in the U.S. Constitution.

Within the guidelines of the U.S. Constitution, Congress—both the House of Representatives and the Senate—passes bills that are either vetoed or signed into law by the President. After the passage of the law, it becomes part of the United States Code, which is the official compilation of federal laws. The state legislatures use a similar process, in which bills become law when signed by the state's governor. Each state has its own official set of laws, some of which are published by the state and some of which are published by commercial publishers. The U.S. Code and the state codes are an important source of legal research; generally, legislators make efforts to make the language of the law as clear as possible.

However, reading the text of a federal or state law generally provides only part of the picture. In the American system of government, after the legislature passes laws and the executive (U.S. President or state governor) signs them, it is up to the judicial branch of the government, the court system, to interpret the laws and decide whether they violate any provision of the Constitution. At the state level, each state's supreme court has the ultimate authority in determining what a law means and whether or not it violates the state constitution. However, the federal courts—headed by the U.S. Supreme Court—can review state laws and court decisions to determine whether they violate federal laws or the U.S. Constitution. For example, a state court may find that a particular criminal law is valid under the state's constitution, but a federal court may then review the state court's decision and determine that the law is invalid under the U.S. Constitution.

It is important, then, to read court decisions when doing legal research. The Constitution uses language that is intentionally very general—for example, prohibiting "unreasonable searches and seizures" by the police—and court cases often provide more guidance. For example, the U.S. Supreme Court's 2001 decision in *Kyllo* v. *United States* held that scanning the outside of a person's house using a heat sensor to determine whether the person is growing marijuana is unreasonable—*if* it is done without a search warrant secured from a judge. Supreme Court decisions provide the most definitive explanation of the law of the land, and it is therefore important to include these in research. Often, when the Supreme Court has not decided a case on a particular issue, a decision by a federal appeals court or a state supreme court can provide guidance; but just as laws and constitutions can vary from state to state, so can federal courts be split on a particular interpretation of federal law or the U.S. Constitution. For example, federal appeals courts in Louisiana and California may reach opposite conclusions in similar cases.

Lawyers and courts refer to statutes and court decisions through a formal system of citations. Use of these citations reveals which court made the decision (or which legislature passed the statute) and when and enables the reader to locate the statute or court case quickly in a law library. For example, the legendary Supreme Court case *Brown* v. *Board of Education* has the legal citation 347 U.S. 483 (1954). At a law library, this 1954 decision can be found on page 483 of volume 347 of the U.S. Reports, the official collection of the Supreme Court's decisions. Citations can also be helpful in locating court cases on the Internet.

Understanding the current state of the law leads only to a partial understanding of the issues covered by the POINT/COUNTERPOINT series. For a fuller understanding of the issues, it is necessary to look at public-policy arguments that the current state of the law is not adequately addressing the issue. Many groups lobby for new legislation or changes to existing legislation; the National Rifle Association (NRA), for example, lobbies Congress and the state legislatures constantly to make existing gun control laws less restrictive and not to pass additional laws. The NRA and other groups dedicated to various causes might also intervene in pending court cases: a group such as Planned Parenthood might file a brief *amicus curiae* (as "a friend of the court")—called an "amicus brief"—in a lawsuit that could affect abortion rights. Interest groups also use the media to influence public opinion, issuing press releases and frequently appearing in interviews on news programs and talk shows. The books in POINT/COUNTERPOINT list some of the interest groups that are active in the issue at hand, but in each case there are countless other groups working at the local, state, and national levels. It is important to read everything with a critical eye, for sometimes interest groups present information in a way that can be read only to their advantage. The informed reader must always look for bias.

Finding sources of legal information on the Internet is relatively simple thanks to "portal" sites such as FindLaw (*www.findlaw.com*), which provides access to a variety of constitutions, statutes, court opinions, law review articles, news articles, and other resources—including all Supreme Court decisions issued since 1893. Other useful sources of information include the U.S. Government Printing Office (*www.gpo.gov*), which contains a complete copy of the U.S. Code, and the Library of Congress's THOMAS system (*thomas.loc.gov*), which offers access to bills pending before Congress as well as recently passed laws. Of course, the Internet changes every second of every day, so it is best to do some independent searching. Most cases, studies, and opinions that are cited or referred to in public debate can be found online— and *everything* can be found in one library or another.

The Internet can provide a basic understanding of most important legal issues, but not all sources can be found there. To find some documents it is necessary to visit the law library of a university or a public law library; some cities have public law libraries, and many library systems keep legal documents at the main branch. On the following page are some common citation forms.

COMMON CITATION FORMS

Source of Law	Sample Citation	Notes
U.S. Supreme Court	*Employment Division v. Smith*, 485 U.S. 660 (1988)	The U.S. Reports is the official record of Supreme Court decisions. There is also an unofficial Supreme Court ("S. Ct.") reporter.
U.S. Court of Appeals	*United States v. Lambert,* 695 F.2d 536 (11th Cir.1983)	Appellate cases appear in the Federal Reporter, designated by "F." The 11th Circuit has jurisdiction in Alabama, Florida, and Georgia.
U.S. District Court	*Carillon Importers, Ltd. v. Frank Pesce Group, Inc.*, 913 F.Supp. 1559 (S.D.Fla.1996)	Federal trial-level decisions are reported in the Federal Supplement ("F. Supp."). Some states have multiple federal districts; this case originated in the Southern District of Florida.
U.S. Code	Thomas Jefferson Commemoration Commission Act, 36 U.S.C., §149 (2002)	Sometimes the popular names of legislation—names with which the public may be familiar—are included with the U.S. Code citation.
State Supreme Court	*Sterling v. Cupp*, 290 Ore. 611, 614, 625 P.2d 123, 126 (1981)	The Oregon Supreme Court decision is reported in both the state's reporter and the Pacific regional reporter.
State Statute	Pennsylvania Abortion Control Act of 1982, 18 Pa. Cons. Stat. 3203-3220 (1990)	States use many different citation formats for their statutes.

143

page:
54: Associated Press Graphics
94: Associated Press Graphics

MARTHA BRIDEGAM, J.D., is a lawyer and freelance writer based in San Francisco. She holds degrees from Harvard University and Hastings College of the Law. She has worked extensively as an advocate for the legal rights of homeless people. Her writing work includes a previous Chelsea House title, *The Right to Privacy*, and magazine contributions on history, politics, and housing regulatory issues. Long-term projects include a landscape history of a site related to the Japanese American internment. She maintains a serious amateur interest in the life and works of George Orwell and is a card-carrying member of the ACLU.

ALAN MARZILLI, M.A., J.D., of Durham, North Carolina, is an independent consultant working on several ongoing projects for state and federal government agencies and nonprofit organizations. He has spoken about mental health issues in thirty states, the District of Columbia, and Puerto Rico; his work includes training mental health administrators, nonprofit management and staff, and people with mental illness and their family members on a wide variety of topics, including effective advocacy, community-based mental health services, and housing. He has written several hand-books and training curricula that are used nationally. He managed statewide and national mental health advocacy programs and worked for several public interest lobbying organizations in Washington, D.C., while studying law at Georgetown University.